FAIR SHARED CITY
GUIDELINES FOR SOCIALLY INCLUSIVE AND GENDER-RESPONSIVE RESIDENTIAL DEVELOPMENT

JANUARY 2022

თბილისის მერია
TBILISI CITY HALL

© 2022 Asian Development Bank
6 ADB Avenue, Mandaluyong City, 1550 Metro Manila, Philippines
Tel +63 2 8632 4444; Fax +63 2 8636 2444
www.adb.org

Some rights reserved. Published in 2022.

ISBN 978-92-9269-339-8 (print); 978-92-9269-340-4 (electronic); 978-92-9269-341-1 (ebook)
Publication Stock No. TIM220012-2
DOI: http://dx.doi.org/10.22617/TIM220012-2

The views expressed in this publication are those of the authors and do not necessarily reflect the views and policies of the Asian Development Bank (ADB) or its Board of Governors or the governments they represent.

ADB does not guarantee the accuracy of the data included in this publication and accepts no responsibility for any consequence of their use. The mention of specific companies or products of manufacturers does not imply that they are endorsed or recommended by ADB in preference to others of a similar nature that are not mentioned.

By making any designation of or reference to a particular territory or geographic area, or by using the term "country" in this document, ADB does not intend to make any judgments as to the legal or other status of any territory or area.

Please contact pubsmarketing@adb.org if you have questions or comments with respect to content, or if you wish to obtain copyright permission for your intended use that does not fall within these terms, or for permission to use the ADB logo.

Corrigenda to ADB publications may be found at http://www.adb.org/publications/corrigenda.

Cover design by Salome Gugunava based on a photo by Gvantsa Nikolaishvili/ADB.

CONTENTS

TABLES, FIGURES, BOXES, AND MAPS

FOREWORD

Making cities more livable is one of the seven operational priorities under Strategy 2030 of the Asian Development Bank (ADB). ADB supports municipalities to make cities safe, inclusive, and sustainable urban centers. It does so by helping cities adopt a holistic approach that includes, among other things, improving services and making them gender-responsive, inclusive, and sustainable; strengthening urban planning by promoting inclusive and participatory processes; and improving urban environments. ADB was pleased to support the Tbilisi City Hall in the preparation of these guidelines as part of this commitment.

Gender-responsive and inclusive design in cities also contributes toward three of the Sustainable Development Goals (SDGs): SDG 5 on achieving gender equality and empowering all women and girls; SDG 11 on making cities and human settlements inclusive, safe, resilient, and sustainable; and SDG 16 on promoting peaceful and inclusive societies for sustainable development. Preparation of practical and applicable tools such as these guidelines helps to build the institutional capacity of municipalities to localize the SDGs to the city level. The Tbilisi City Hall was supported in these efforts by drawing from the depth and breadth of experience of Vienna City Hall in mainstreaming gender in urban planning. Gender-responsive design makes women feel safe in the city and enables them to carry out their daily activities and enjoy its amenities. A woman-friendly city is, by default, a city that is friendly to children and the elderly.

Support for the preparation of these guidelines through ADB Trust Funds builds on several years of partnership with Tbilisi City administration in urban planning, and urban transport initiatives. The partnership continues to flourish through the Livable Cities Investment Program to improve planning and infrastructure in major cities and regional clusters in Georgia, including in the capital city of Tbilisi. These guidelines will contribute to ensuring the promotion of gender-responsiveness and inclusiveness of initiatives under this program.

I hope the insights this publication offers will provide cross-regional learning to foster innovative urban development across Asia and the Pacific, to meet the evolving needs and interests of all.

Bruno Carrasco
Director General
Sustainable Development and Climate Change Department
Asian Development Bank

MESSAGE

Tbilisi is one of the largest and most urbanized cities in Georgia. The city is home to people from diverse national, ethnic, and religious backgrounds. People of all ages, gender identities, and sexual orientations, each have their own diverse mix of interests and occupations. The capital provides a wealth of employment and educational opportunities, and a broad range of housing, cultural, and recreation options. Such diversity ensures that in everyday life of this historic capital continues to be vibrant and dynamic.

The population is highly concentrated in many residential districts and neighborhoods of Tbilisi. This produces a favorable environment to provide services, foster creativity, and enable the growth of economic activity. The best outcomes for the people and for the city are when everyone, regardless of their sex, religion, ethnicity, or age, and including those with disabilities, can contribute to, and benefit from, all of the social and economic opportunities that Tbilisi offers. One of the biggest challenges facing the city is balancing the different needs and priorities of the diverse population to ensure high-quality, inclusive development and a harmonious and peaceful society.

Development of a high-quality livable environment is equally important in central districts as well as the outskirts of the city. Strategies for carefully increasing the density have to be selected for central districts; strategies for sustainable and compact development where services can be effectively provided have to be selected for the outskirts of the city. Tbilisi is growing rapidly, and city planners and the mayor's office need to carefully ensure that all groups can live together peacefully in quality environments that provide for their different needs. The major guiding principle is for a fair shared city. This principle is based on the practice of gender-sensitive planning that has already been used in the city of Vienna, Austria for many years.

These guidelines are developed based on the experience of Vienna, and provide gender-sensitive planning criteria for city planners and various departments of the Tbilisi City Mayor's Office. The guidelines will play a crucial role in balancing diverse needs during planning and ensuring gender-sensitive decision-making processes. I hope these guidelines will provide valuable input for planning offices, developers and the municipality staff. Our common goal is to ensure a high quality of life in our beautiful capital.

Marika Darchia
Deputy Chair, Tbilisi City Assembly
Chair, Gender Council
16 September 2021

ACKNOWLEDGMENTS

These guidelines are the result of the collaborative efforts of the Asian Development Bank (ADB) and the Transport and Urban Development Agency of Tbilisi City Hall.

The core team from ADB

Gillian Brown, lead consultant
Nana Adeishvili, project manager
Gvantsa Nikolaishvili, national urban planning specialist
Eva Kail, gender planning expert

The core team from the Transport and Urban Development Agency of Tbilisi City Hall:

Giorgi Maisuradze, Irakli Mtskhvetadze, and **Elisabed Archvadze;**
Nano Zazanashvili and **Tata Verulashvili** (former employees of the Urban Development Department)

ADB Project Team

Samantha Hung, chief of Gender Equality Thematic Group
Prabhjot Khan, social development specialist (Gender and Development),
    Sustainable Development and Climate Change Department (SDCC)
Ramola Naik Singru, principal urban development specialist,
    Central and West Asia Department
Ann Mushayt Alemania, associate operations analyst, SDCC

Production

Salome Gugunava, graphic and cover designer/architect
Teona Begishvili, editor and corrector
Tornike Lortkiphanidze, publication designer
Neli Akobia, translator

The core team thanks the following for their support, in-depth interviews, comments, reviews, and technical inputs.

Transport and Urban Development Agency and former Urban Development Department staff

Viktor Tsilosani, Davit Jaiani, Nini Bagashvili, Otar Chitidze, Sandro Togonidze (former head of the Urban Development Department), **Giorgi Ebanoidze** (former head of the Urban Development Department), **David Asanidze** (former employee of the Urban Development Department), **Vajha Chkadua, Giorgi Basiladze, Mari Natsvlishvili, Luka Kikiani, Teona Etsetadze, Eka Madzgarashvili, Mariam Tavadze** (former employee), **Ana Pheradze**

Architects and Other Experts

Mariam Lomidze, Nutsa Nadareishvili, Bela Tinikashvili, Tamar Katsitadze, Ana Khurodze, Elene Khundadze, Liudmila Chikovani, Shota Demetrashvili, Nika Gogeshvili, Keti Kobulia, Giorgi Makharashvili, Vaja Kukhianidze, Tamar Getsadze (Educational and Scientific Infrastructure Development Agency), **Zaza Chichua** (Agency for Kindergartens of Tbilisi), Nutsa Pruidze (UNICEF Georgia)

Developers and Company Directors

Tornike Abuladze (director, Arsi), **Beso Jikurauli** (former director, AS Georgia Dirsi), **Lin Tao** (deputy head of the general director, Hualing Group), **Nikoloz Gelenidze** (head, Engineering Department, Hualing Group)

Asian Development Bank

Sonomi Tanaka, country director, Lao People's Democratic Republic Resident Mission
Shane Rosenthal, country director, Georgia Resident Mission
Yong Ye, country director, Pakistan Resident Mission
Hiranya Mukhopadhyay, chief of governance thematic group, SDCC
Heeyoung Hong, principal urban development specialist (Finance), Central and West Asia Department
Laxmi Sharma, urban development specialist, South Asia Department
Rachana Shrestha, public management specialist, SDCC
Tea Papuashvili, associate project officer (Infrastructure), Georgia Resident Mission

ABBREVIATIONS

ADB	–	Asian Development Bank
FAR	–	floor area ratio
GeoStat	–	National Statistics Office of Georgia
ha	–	hectare
LUMP	–	land use master plan
m	–	meter
mm	–	millimeter
m²	–	square meter
SDG	–	Sustainable Development Goal
SNIP	–	Construction Norms and Rules
TBT	–	Tbilisi Bus Transit
TUDA	–	Tbilisi Transport and Urban Development Agency

1

INTRODUCTION

1.1   Background and Purpose

These guidelines are intended for use by urban planners, architects, and persons interested in residential development in Tbilisi. The objective is to support parties involved in the planning and design process to develop decisions that are functionally, spatially, and socially well-integrated into the existing urban environment and where the needs of various groups of varying ages, sexes, and social roles as well as social, cultural, and physical abilities are considered on an equal basis.

This publication, *Fair Shared City: Guidelines for Socially Inclusive and Gender-Responsive Residential Development,* was developed within the framework of the Asian Development Bank (ADB) project Future Cities Future Women.[1] The document was developed through a cooperation between Tbilisi City Hall and local and international experts involved in the project for 2 years. This document is the first attempt at compiling the practical guidelines tailored to the characteristics of urban development in Tbilisi that will support the formation of a human rights-focused, fair, inclusive, and gender-responsive residential environment.

The guidelines take into account both local and international strategic documents, including the Land Use Master Plan of Tbilisi, the United Nations Sustainable Development Goals (SDGs) and the memorandum of understanding signed between United Nations Children's Fund (UNICEF) Georgia and Tbilisi City Hall on the initiative to develop child-friendly cities. The guidelines refer to SDGs 5, 11, and 16, which touch on topics such as gender equality; inclusive, safe, resilient, and sustainable development; establishment of responsible and inclusive institutional systems, etc. In addition, the document was developed based on the analysis of the legal acts regulating city planning, construction in general, and related fields.

1.2   The Need for Guidelines

The developed territory of Tbilisi is actively growing and new residential complexes are being built in all districts. Considering the rapid development and the lack of documents regulating the field, Tbilisi faces challenges such as ensuring a quality living environment, green spaces, infrastructure, basic services, health care, education, quality employment, and safety.
The morphology and the capacity of the traffic system are additional challenges.

The situation with an incoherent planning system is a complex one, both on the national and city levels. The standards of the former Soviet Union influenced by the Central European planning tradition are still valid on paper, while newer regulations and criteria are much more oriented on the American planning system. The Tbilisi City Hall, with its limited planning capacity, has to face

---

[1]   ADB. 2014. *Technical Assistance for Promoting Gender Equality and Women's Empowerment Phase 2.* Manila (TA 8797-REG); and ADB. 2017. Technical Assistance for Strengthening Institutions for Localizing Agenda 2030 for Sustainable Development. Manila (TA 9387-REG).

dynamics in the building sector and urban development projects of private investors wishing for quick approval of their detailed development plans, while sometimes facing poor-quality proposals. Due to the lack of methodologically coherent guidelines, outcomes of the design process are unpredictable and the process of consultation is unclear.

The existing standards and legislation include some vague statements that are difficult to utilize in practice. When planning residential developments in Georgia, the development floor area ratio (FAR) is used as the main guiding indicator. Other quantitative and qualitative indicators are paid less attention. When attempting to implement other assessment indicators such as population density, questions arise on how to count the population, what the minimum residential space is per inhabitant, which standards should be regarded as guiding, and what is high density in general.

The methodology developed within these guidelines represents an attempt to reconcile quantitative and qualitative approaches to design criteria based, on the one hand, on existing national standards and legislation, and international standards on the other. This will then simplify the planning and design process to enable the formation of a healthy urban environment.

1.3   Procedures and Methodology

A comparative analysis of existing standards and norms in Vienna and Tbilisi was conducted. Vienna is recognized as a leader in mainstreaming gender in urban planning and development and the goal was to integrate the principles and criteria provided in the Viennese guidelines on gender mainstreaming in urban planning and urban development into Tbilisi urban planning practice.[2] Work meetings and workshops were conducted in Tbilisi and Vienna within the frames of which main planning criteria were selected for developing fair shared living spaces. Field visits were conducted in both Tbilisi and Vienna. Municipal staff and international experts visited large urban projects and talked with developers and company directors. While working on the guidelines, interviews was held with different stakeholders in both public and private sectors. The information gathered from interviews were used to develop the vision and criteria for a residential neighborhood. In addition, practicing architects provided regular assessments on the content of the guidelines.

To localize the gender-sensitive planning criteria, detailed development plans in Tbilisi were assessed and a more detailed urban analysis was conducted in one of the residential rayons chosen as the study area. When selecting the study area, attention was mainly paid to the areas with high-quality residential environment and infrastructure that can be used as a minimum standard in other districts of the city. Vake residential rayon was selected as the study area as the quality of its urban structures is recognized citywide. It also offered different typologies of building and block structures from different periods. It is important to note that the main part of Vake district was planned according to the standards in contrast to the current urban

2   City of Vienna. 2013. *Gender Mainstreaming in Urban Planning and Urban Development*. www.wein.gv.at/stadtenwicklung/ studien/pdf/b008358.pdf.

development process. The proposed urban parameters have been analyzed and tested for this study area. Vienna has done a similar analysis for its three largest and most important urban development areas, using the parameters of the gender planning manual.

Within the frames of the analysis, spatial and legal data were gathered from various agencies through written and verbal communication.[3] Based on the collected data, the existing urban structure within the study area as well as its characteristics were assessed; and planning units of various levels (districts and blocks), population density, demographic make-up as per age and gender or sex, location, area, and coverage areas were identified. In addition, the location of social infrastructure as well as their coverage areas, various economic activities, and accessibility of public transportation were assessed and identified. Several field visits were also conducted.

The study area covers only a small part of the city; therefore, it was only possible to conduct a detailed analysis on certain components at neighborhood and district levels. For example, in the case of green spaces, the park coverage analysis only allowed for assessment of the local situation. As for the green spaces in residential rayons and the city center, an additional study would need to be conducted across the city.

With the goal to assess some criteria in more detail in Vake residential rayon, a more detailed analysis was conducted in one of the residential blocks on green spaces and the current indicators for playgrounds, shading of shared concentrated green spaces, and access to social infrastructure and public transportation stops. An assessment tool was prepared and used in the study (Appendix 1), and several maps of Vake district were produced (Appendix 2).

1.4   Key Resources

The Vienna Guidelines on Gender Mainstreaming in Urban Planning and Urban Development were used as the main conceptual framework for the present document (footnote 2).

The document was also developed based on legislation regulating city construction, construction in general, and related fields. These include the following:

- Major Regulations on the Usage and Development of Settled Territories, Decree 59 of the Government of Georgia, signed on 15 January 2014;

- Regulations on the Usage and Development of Tbilisi Municipality Territories, Decree 14-39 of the Tbilisi City Municipality Assembly, enacted on 24 May 2016; and

---

3   GeoStat; Ministry of Education and Science of Georgia, Agency for Kindergartens of Tbilisi, Department of Culture, Education, Sports and Youth Affairs, Ministry of Economy and Sustainable Development of Georgia, Ministry of Regional Development and Infrastructure of Georgia, Emergency Management Service, District Governments of Tbilisi Municipality.

- Land Use Master Plan of The Capital City, Decree 39-18 of the Tbilisi City Municipality Assembly approved on 15 March 2019. March 15, 2019 Decree N39-18 by Tbilisi Municipality Assembly on "the Land Use Master Plan of the Capital City."

The document also draws on and should be read alongside the following ADB guidelines and toolkits:

- Enabling Inclusive Cities: Toolkit for Inclusive Urban Development,[4]

- Green City Development Toolkit,[5] and

- Creating Livable Asian Cities.[6]

A full list of relevant documents and additional information can be found in the References section.

1.5   Structure of the Document

The structure of these guidelines follows the planning logic. The discussion starts off from the vision and planning principles of a residential neighborhood that establish the theoretical framework conditions in the planning process. Criteria are provided thematically in line with the vision and principles. Each criterion contains several thematic parts. At the end of the document, there is a questionnaire and an assessment matrix that enable city planners and municipality staff to check adherence to the criteria provided in the guidelines. The assessment matrix provides an opportunity to assess the technical part of the document, whereas the questionnaire provides an opportunity to assess the qualitative part of the project proposal.

1.6   Future Guidelines Development

These guidelines were prepared alongside the *Fair Shared Green and Recreational Spaces: Guidelines for Gender-Responsive and Inclusive Design*, and also the *Inclusive Urban Area Guidelines*.[7] These three documents together start to provide a framework for inclusive and gender-responsive design in urban areas. However, planning and building guidelines and standards are constantly being refined, and these guidelines should be treated as living iterative documents that can evolve and be added to over time.

---

4   ADB. 2017. Enabling Inclusive Cities: ToolKit for Inclusive Urban Development. https://www.adb.org/documents/enabling-inclusive-cities.

5   ADB. 2015. *Green City Development Toolkit*. https://www.adb.org/sites/default/files/institutional-document/173693/green-city-dev-toolkit.pdf.

6   ADB. 2021. Creating Livable Asian Cities. https://www.adb.org/publications/creating-livable-asian-cities.

7   ADB and Tbilisi City Hall. 2021. *Fair Shared Green and Recreational Spaces: Guidelines for Gender-Responsive and Inclusive Design*. Manila: Asian Development Bank; and ADB and Government of Georgia, Ministry of Regional Development and Infrastructure. Forthcoming. Inclusive Urban Area Guidelines. Manila: Asian Development Bank.

2

VISION FOR
A FAIR SHARED CITY

The urban structure supports and determines the quality of everyday life. In urban development processes, planning and design often have to juggle competing interests. Our decision-making follows the principles of a fair shared city.

2.1 What Is a Fair Shared City?

A fair shared city for everybody is a human city where, in the development and planning processes, the user patterns of all different groups are taken into account in a holistic manner. This requires identifying different user groups and their different needs, and translating these needs in technical criteria that contribute to the planning discourse. A fair shared city is both gender-responsive and inclusive. Gender-responsive cities take account of the different gender roles, behaviors, opportunities, and consequences of power differences between women and men, and girls and boys. An inclusive city is built on (i) joint strategic visions of all stakeholders through a participatory planning and decision-making process incorporating universal design, integrated urban planning, transparent accountability mechanisms, and the use of the city's inherent assets; (ii) knowledge and information sharing; (iii) public participation and contribution; (iv) mechanisms, such as cross-subsidies, social protection, and gender balance, to ensure an adequate standard of living to the most economically disadvantaged and vulnerable population; (v) geographical and social mobility; (vi) business environment and pro-poor financing services that attract capital investment and allow everybody the possibility to undertake economic activities; (vii) resilience to global environmental and socioeconomic shocks and threats; and (viii) mechanisms to ensure the sustainable use of its resources (footnote 5).

Following the goals and methods of a fair shared city necessitates a systematic quality assessment of equal opportunities for different user groups that lead to fair and efficient use of public resources and a higher-quality urban environment.

The most important distinction under urban development aspects is the orientation of different user groups in the local neighborhood and their dependence on its quality. In the definition of user groups, these guidelines use the Gender Plus concept. Besides sexes, the guidelines also differentiate between carers and takers, life phases and age groups, cultural patterns, and social backgrounds. All these groups and their daily lives differ—their workload in paid and unpaid work, their incomes, their leisure interests and mobility conditions and patterns, their fear of crime, and their likelihood to be exposed to violence and sexual harassment.

Integrating the fair shared city planning principles into these first comprehensive planning guidelines is an important step for a social, sustainable, and resilient planning culture. Tbilisi is the first city in the world to do so. Even in Vienna, such coherent planning guidelines with integrated gender aspects do not yet exist.

2.2 Gender-Responsive Planning

Over the decades, cities were mostly designed for full-time employed people and little attention was paid to the spatial needs of other users, especially those with unpaid caregiving roles. The transportation system, residential districts, and public spaces were planned with the same logic. An unpaid caregiver's everyday routine differs significantly from the conventional live–work–play concept. Their everyday activities take place primarily in local urban spaces and include locally focused activities. For example, taking children to school, shopping, taking elderly people to appointments, and so on. They often work part-time. They have different needs for transportation, functional distribution, public spaces, and street network planning. They walk and use public transportation more often. Empirical observation shows that unpaid work is mostly done by women, while men mostly work full-time jobs. Furthermore, in Tbilisi, at 63%, the majority of public transport users are women.[8]

In addition to people engaged in unpaid care work and people working part-time, the target groups mostly using the local urban spaces include elderly persons over the age of 75 years. Their ability to move around and engage in activities greatly decreases with the increasing age and deterioration of their health condition. The noted target groups also include children younger than 12 years old who need to be accompanied by carers.

Imbalance in city planning in terms of gender, age, and social groups leads to a sense of injustice and makes life much more difficult for many. This imbalance can be mitigated by using a gender-responsive planning approach. Many cities in Europe have already established this methodology including Vienna, where gender mainstreaming in urban planning was first implemented in 1992 (Box 2.1).

Box 2.1: Gender Mainstreaming in Urban Planning in Vienna

Gender mainstreaming in urban planning in Vienna has a long history. In 2019, Vienna topped the Mercer quality of living city ranking.[a] Human scale, focus on open and green spaces, decent housing environment, personal safety, and quality-oriented planning process distinguish Vienna from many other advanced cities.

Gender mainstreaming is well-established as a central strategic discipline in urban planning in Vienna, and is used in various strategic urban planning and sector strategies. Over 50 pilot projects have been implemented in Vienna and have demonstrated the possibilities and benefits of this approach in urban planning. Their experiences are summarized in the manual on Gender Mainstreaming in Urban Planning and Urban Development, which was used as a resource in the preparation of the Tbilisi City guidelines.[b]

---

[a]   Mercer. Quality of Living City Ranking. https://mobilityexchange.mercer.com/insights/quality-of-living-rankings.
[b]   City of Vienna. 2013. *Gender Mainstreaming in Urban Planning and Urban Development*. https://www.wien.gv.at/stadtentwicklung/studien/pdf/b008358.pdf.
Source: Authors.

---

[8]   Systra. 2016. *Consulting Services for Organization of a Transportation Household Survey in Tbilisi Metropolitan area*. ADB, Municipal Development Fund of Georgia, and Tbilisi City Hall.https://tbilisi.gov.ge/img/original/2018/4/20/THS_Final_Report_Eng.pdf.

Gender-responsive planning considers the needs of those who are often overlooked in the planning process. Thus gender-, age- and group-specific interests are systematically considered and the impact on these interests is systematically assessed at each stage in the planning process. The main objective lies in meeting demands for space by individual groups, creating safer, more flexible, and adaptable, and fairly (objectively) distributed spaces. Gender-sensitive planning informs planners about the everyday needs of different groups and enables them to be more aware about the diversity of their target groups. It also helps planners to see problems not seen before and thus be able to respond to them. Gender-sensitive planning supports the multidisciplinary planning process, as well as methodological innovation.

2.3 Well-Balanced Density and Human Scale Orientation

A carefully chosen density of the built environment with mixed structures and functionality follows the principles of a city with short distances and favorable conditions for public transport, social infrastructure, and shopping facilities; and contributes to a feeling of urbanity. In a city that has high walkability, high connectivity, and sustainable public transport, residents are not dependent on private vehicles. This is especially important for poorer people. It also has a positive impact on the environment and climate if car use is reduced due to the availability and quality of public transport. A certain density of buildings helps to increase visibility among occupants and passers by, and raises social control and the feeling of safety. It is also a precondition for day care facilities and primary schools within walking distance and hence, supports carers for children.

At the same time, balanced urban structure is very important as good architecture cannot compensate for bad urban planning and design. Therefore, it is also necessary to provide enough open space. A human scale of building dimension and block structure in the tradition of towns within the region has to be preserved to create a feeling of an attractive neighborhood and contribute to good quality of life for locally orientated or vulnerable groups. Achieving this vision is possible through semi-closed block structure (Figure 2.1).

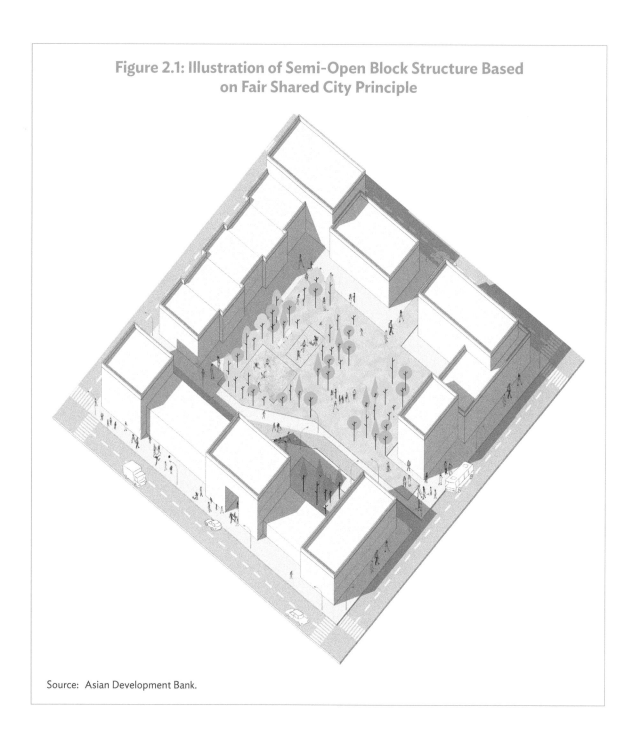

Figure 2.1: Illustration of Semi-Open Block Structure Based on Fair Shared City Principle

Source: Asian Development Bank.

2.4 Quality of Life in Residential Areas

A user-friendly and human orientation of urban design considers the needs of all age groups, people with disabilities, and people doing domestic and care work. An enabling environment and the availability of shopping and health facilities, day care facilities, and schools nearby are necessary to support work–life balance. Safe walking conditions raise the autonomy of children and reduce care work.

The physical environment is built to a human scale in regard to the height of buildings and pedestrian-orientated streets and squares. There are well-integrated open and green spaces of all sizes. Newly developed residential areas are inclusive and inviting. Public, semi-public, and private spaces are clearly defined by shape and design. Only a few fences are necessary—borders are not aggressive, but can be distinguished This creates good interconnectivity of the different spheres. The connectivity of public spaces and the ground floors is high as well.

The inclusive focus shows up in the quality of public and semi-public space for pedestrians and public transport users. The universal design of a public space means that sidewalks are suitable for the disabled, the elderly, and people with small children. Sidewalks that have a high usability for wheelchairs, prams, and trolleys also contribute to comfort for all walkers. The presence of trees that provide shade and availability of drinking water increase the amenity in the streets. For some people, strategically placed sitting facilities are not only an amenity, but a precondition for their mobility, as they have the need for frequent rest. Trees improve the microclimate, as do the aquifer areas and unsealed open ground and green roofs and facades. Avoiding or reducing urban heat islands is especially important for vulnerable groups such as small children, old or sick people, or people with low income in cramped living conditions.

3

PLANNING PRINCIPLES AND OBJECTIVES

3.1 Fair Shared City

The fair shared city is a principle of planning which caters equally to the interests of various groups in the city, provides equal access to public goods, and seeks to eliminate inequality and discrimination, as well as prevent the adverse impact of planning arrangements on individual groups.

This principle acknowledges that there are different groups living in cities and that they have varying needs, interests, and life circumstances. The daily lives of men and women, girls and boys, and their behavioral models differ at various stages of life, social and cultural backgrounds, gender identities, or physical abilities. Development focused on the local community and specific groups within it (children, young people, elderly citizens, and caretakers) is of special importance. Therefore, the impact of planning on each of these groups has to be considered when developing planning solutions for city construction.

This illustration is an urban environment where all social, gender, and age groups are considered
(Photo by Gvantsa Nikolaishvili/ADB).

The objectives of the planning principle are the following:

- regularly check the level of fairness in planning for the needs of various groups to resolve emerging differences in needs and priorities at various stages of planning;

- develop a well-integrated urban structure to avoid functional and physical isolation of new neighborhoods;

- develop a city with short distances for daily travel;

- create accessible, safe, and comfortable public spaces and neighborhood or district infrastructure adapted to the needs of all groups, which will help children, young people, the elderly, and persons with specific needs to move around independently and comfortably in public spaces, thus reducing the workload of parents and caretakers;

- create public spaces where safety is achieved through social control, with well-lit roads, sidewalks and footpaths for pedestrians, as well as entrances with a high level of visibility from public spaces; and

- ensure a good location, adequate open space or area with good accessibility for the projected areas for schools, kindergartens, and other elements of social infrastructure.

More details of design features and standards for ensuring urban areas are inclusive and accessible for people of all ages and abilities can be found in the Inclusive Urban Area Guidelines.[9]

3.2 Compact and Connected City

The compact and connected city is a principle of planning that implies formation or development of a high-quality, dense, but well-balanced urban structure using inner city resources. It aims to prevent the growth of municipal expenditure, as well as to ensure sustainable urban mobility and ecological sustainability.

Priorities within the planning process include the following: development of territories with combined functions and formation of neighborhoods where high-quality social infrastructure, recreational spaces, and everyday services are located within walking distance. Functions that are important for the city are equally distributed and evenly situated throughout the whole territory of the city and the residents travel using comfortable, prompt, accessible, and inclusive public transportation or other nonmotorized means of transportation.

---

[9]   ADB and Government of Georgia, Ministry of Regional Development and Infrastructure. Forthcoming. Inclusive Urban Area Guidelines. Manila: Asian Development Bank.

The objectives of the planning principle are the following:

- avoid urban expansion and utilization of undeveloped territories around the city for new construction;

- utilize former industrial areas within the developed territory of the city;

- promote polycentric development;

- develop urban structure focused on public transportation that will reduce dependence on private vehicles for transportation; and

- develop neighborhoods where recreational areas, as well as social and daily services are located within walking distance.

3.3 Green City

Green city is a principle of planning which includes improvement of recreational conditions as well as conditions for the protection of the environment in the capital.[10]

Its goal is to strictly adhere to the requirements in terms of protection, restoration, and development of natural landscapes and ecosystems, as well as open and recreational spaces in the city. The goal of this principle is also to ensure formation of high-quality and safe recreational spaces available or accessible to everybody and adapted to the interests of groups with diverse needs.

This principle recognizes that the natural environment and the recreational areas of the capital are the main elements of personal and social well-being. It promotes social integration and has an important impact on the physical health of citizens; therefore, urban planning arrangements should ensure protection and development of this principle, as well as an adequate number of high-quality recreational areas.

The objectives of the green city planning principle are the following:

- create connected green recreational systems in the form of a unified network of Mtkvari riverbed and valleys connecting individual natural and green areas;

- create a safe and healthy living environment by modernizing ecologically harmful and technologically obsolete enterprises and developing green buffer zones between these enterprises and residential areas;

---

10   S. Sandhu et al. 2016. *GREEEN Solutions for Livable Cities*. Manila: Asian Development Bank. https://www.adb.org/sites/default/files/publication/181442/greeen-solutions-livable-cities.pdf.

- increase the area of green and open spaces for general usage in the developed part of the city;

- develop safe squares and public spaces adapted to the needs of all social groups in each district and neighborhood; and

- support a good balance of shady and sunny areas at the block level through urban design.

3.4 Resilient City

Urban resilience is the ability of a city to survive, adapt, and grow, despite all possible factors of stress and shock. Outdated infrastructure, air pollution, earthquakes, and other natural threats are challenges that the capital should take into consideration and address when making planning decisions.

Decisions on urban construction should be focused on preventing and mitigating damage caused by natural hazards and associated risks. New development should not deteriorate living conditions and the state of the public and engineering infrastructure, but rather improve it as much as possible.

The objectives of the urban resilience planning principle are the following:

- identify areas and valleys with a high risk of natural hazards, as well as flooding areas, areas with a high risk of landslides, etc., and limit development opportunities for construction purposes in these areas;

- form a safe and healthy living environment and protect it from harmful impact, including consideration of sanitation and hygiene conditions;

- consider the requirements of engineering–utility infrastructure when developing city construction projects; and

- support rehabilitation of deteriorating houses and apartments and protect them against further deterioration, including housing and apartments in the historical part of Tbilisi, in accordance with its historical, cultural, artistic, and social values.

4

PLANNING CRITERIA AND METHODOLOGICAL GUIDELINES

4.1 Well-Balanced Density and Mixed-Use Development

When urban structures with well-balanced density and are mixed use are developed and a principle of a compact and interconnected city is taken into account, and it is effectively connected with other parts of the city by public transportation, such neighborhoods constitute an organic part of the city system and city resources are optimally used. Mixed-use neighborhoods include residential buildings, job sites, commercial sites, schools, kindergartens, and recreational spaces with sufficient capacity located at walking distance, close to one another. Such a compact distribution of various functions in a residential neighborhood ensures that the everyday needs of inhabitants are met. It also increases their sense of safety and social control and prevents the creation of urban heat islands.

Dense monofunctional residential areas without mixed-use development depend on other neighborhoods for the different uses necessary for residential areas. This increases the necessity of frequent long-distance travel and promotes car dependency.

A well-balanced density is one of the preconditions of sustainable urban development. Effective usage of the city's land resources supports the prevention of urban sprawl and suburbanization. High-density development on a developed territory is much more cost-effective in ensuring municipal services as well as social, engineering, and transportation infrastructure.[11] Shopping facilities also depend on their frequency in the streets.

In well-designed urban development with well-balanced density and high concentration of people, sufficient public transport can be provided effectively. This helps to reduce the dependence on cars and leads to an improvement of the ecological condition (Example 1).

However, there is also the possibility of "density-fuelled stress," caused mainly by over-exceeded FAR and massive or high-rise buildings with high population density and inadequate spatial planning arrangements (footnote 2). Insufficient open and green spaces, heavy traffic, a multitude of open parking spaces at the ground level, and lack of local social infrastructure which require walking or traveling long distances are additional factors. Such developments are characterized by the lack of ventilation and sunlight in both external and internal spaces, loaded facades, and odor and noise due to car traffic. The lack of open and green spaces makes it difficult to organize areas that are well-adapted to the needs of various groups. As a result, the population is gathered in a few locations for recreational purposes, resulting in noise and discomfort for both local residents and users of open spaces (Example 2).

---

[11]   UN-Habitat. A New Strategy of Sustainable Neighbourhood Planning: Five principles. https://unhabitat.org/a-new-strategy-of-sustainable-neighbourhood-planning-five-principles-0.(accessed 21 May 2021).

Aerial view. Well-balanced density within the semi-closed block on the crossroad of Vaja-pshavela and Pekini avenues (photo by Tbilisi City Hall).

City scape. Over-exceeded FAR and "density-fuelled stress" in the so-called district of "Akademkalaki" (photo by Tbilisi City Hall).

The side effects of excessive density and monofunctional residential buildings have a big impact on people engaged in care work, persons with disability, elderly persons, and women and men who are engaged in unpaid work at home. Typically they might need to travel long distances to access district sites for everyday needs, which often exceed the norm for the coverage area (sections 4.3, 4.4, 4.5, and 4.6), resulting in a deterioration in the quality of life. Insufficient or low-quality public schools and kindergartens in the neighborhood can lead to overcrowding and cause parents to take children to school or kindergarten in other neighborhoods, which increases their time burden. Elderly persons and people with restricted mobility may stay at home or walk on adjacent streets rather than travel to recreation spaces if they are not easily accessible (Boxes 4.1 and 4.2).

Box 4.1: Pedestrian Accessibility of the Elderly to Parks

The urban analysis conducted in the study area in Vake district revealed that only in 56.6% of the developed part of the district could pedestrians access parks and recreational spaces for elderly persons living within 250 meters from their home. As much as 46% of elderly persons living on the remaining territory live a bit farther away from parks. For many of them, it is not easy to walk or otherwise travel long distances and therefore, they often prefer to stay at home.

Sources: Tbilisi Transport and Urban Development Agency and ADB.

Box 4.2: Pedestrian Accessibility Analysis of the Public Schools and Kindergartens

The urban analysis conducted in Vake district revealed that normal pedestrian access areas at existing public schools (750 meters) and kindergartens (300 meters) were available in only 55% of the developed territory for public schools and 12% for kindergartens. This means that children living in the remaining territory have little access to the adequate social infrastructure and have to walk or travel long distances. The analysis revealed that the lack of public schools and kindergartens is mainly a problem in districts that have been developed relatively later on and where the construction processes were not well-organized. Today, these districts are characterized by high density.

Sources: Tbilisi Transport and Urban Development Agency and ADB.

4.1.1 Density Indicators

The density parameter is an important spatial tool that supports planners and decision makers in managing land use planning.

There are several main indicators that are recommended for measuring density: development density or floor area ratio (FAR) per hectare (ha), as well as population density (person/ha) and residential density (dwelling unit/ha) (Figure 4.1).

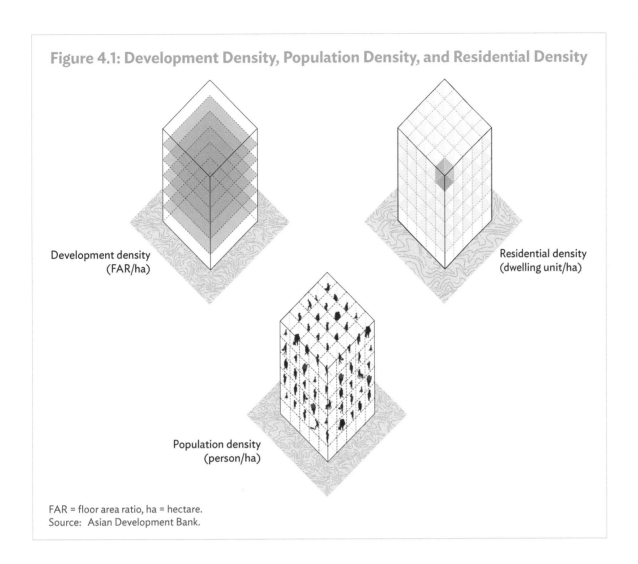

Figure 4.1: Development Density, Population Density, and Residential Density

Development density
(FAR/ha)

Residential density
(dwelling unit/ha)

Population density
(person/ha)

FAR = floor area ratio, ha = hectare.
Source: Asian Development Bank.

Each density indicator is calculated individually. Density is identified by dividing the total floor area, the number of persons (residents), and dwelling units by the area of the territory. The area of the territory is measured in hectares.

The FAR along with the number of dwelling units to be built are important indicators for developers and architects in the planning process, while the expected number, age structure and territorial distribution (density) of the potential new population represent important information for the municipality in providing municipal services and ensuring even urban development. Residential density includes the density of dwelling units and population along with the FAR, but one indicator does not automatically define the other. For example, in a high-density urban development, if large dwelling units are planned, then it will have a lower density of dwelling units and population. That is why all three indicators should be paid equal attention to at all stages of planning (Figure 4.2).

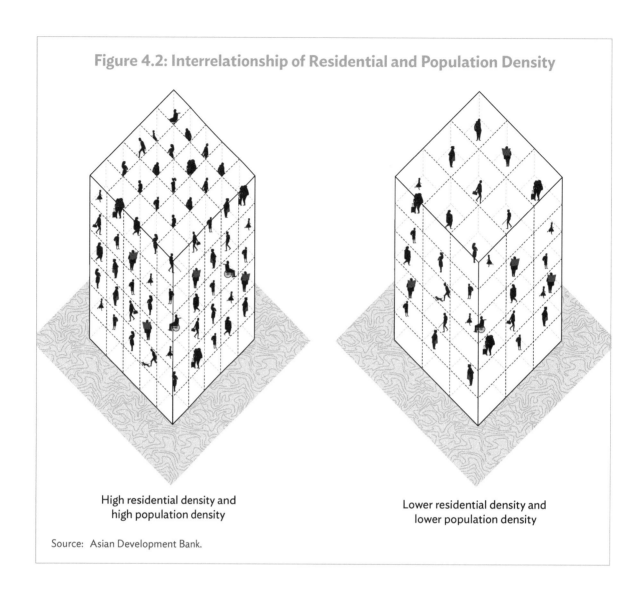

Figure 4.2: Interrelationship of Residential and Population Density

High residential density and
high population density

Lower residential density and
lower population density

Source: Asian Development Bank.

When analyzing density or developing a project proposal, gross and net territorial indicators also have to be considered.[12]

The gross indicator is calculated for the whole project site, which includes both residential and non-residential buildings (schools, kindergarten and so on) together with open spaces (semi-public parks, streets and so on); while the net indicator is calculated only for areas designated for residential use and is restricted to the land plots where the residential buildings are placed.

---

12   Government of Georgia.2019. On the Rules for Developing Spatial and City Planning Documentation. Decree No. 260. Annex 8 states that "Gross indicator is the indicator related to the residential area which fully includes transport infrastructure, recreational functions, and daily and socio-cultural service sites needed for quality life along with residential buildings." "Net indicator relates to the residential area which includes the needed minimum functions for residents (pathways, greenery, small sports and children's fields, open parking lots, etc.) within the cadastral unit of the residential building(s) together with the residential building itself.

Tbilisi's urban planning legislation only offers the net indicators for FAR.[13]

Therefore, it is crucial that net and gross areas are distinguished on the project site and that FAR is applied only to the net area to ensure proper development.

This way, it is possible to achieve a more balanced development. As for the dwelling unit and population density, they are both used for the net and gross areas. But the number of people and population density is mostly calculated on the gross area.

4.1.1.1 Floor Area Ratio

The maximum FAR for a development in Tbilisi (as per the functional zones defined in the land use master plan) and the rules for its calculation are provided in the "Regulations on the usage and development of territories in Tbilisi municipality."[14]

As noted, the FAR defines the total area of ground and above-ground floors in a building allowed on a specific land plot in a specific zone. Accordingly, this is meant as a net density indicator and it can be considered only in case of individual land plots. As a rule, the net density indicator of one land plot is higher than the gross density indicator of the residential area/block or neighborhood.

The maximum FAR for an individual land plot in a high density residential neighborhood in Tbilisi is 2.5 (footnote 15). When development takes place using the maximum FAR, it is important to produce a balanced planning solution that includes considerations for the adequate number of floors and dimensions of the building (section 4.2.3), sufficient space for playgrounds and open spaces (section 4.5.1), sufficient sunlight (section 4.2.4), and access to the main functions (section 4.3).

If the FAR is higher than 2.0, a careful quality assessment is very important. Where the FAR is below 2.0, a high housing quality is very likely safeguarded (footnote 2). It should be noted that in Vienna, the urban planning and design process is complex. FAR is only an additional tool used for assessment to give an orientation in strategic planning documents or at the beginning of the urban design process, but is not fixed in legally binding planning documents.

According to the land use master plan, when planning large urban developments, discussion starts with the functional zones and their development intensity coefficients. The maximum net FAR given by the land use master plan is often mistakenly used as a maximum FAR for the whole urban development site prior to the spatial arrangement of the area.

---

[13]   Tbilisi City Assembly. 2016. Regulations on the Usage and Development of Territories in Tbilisi Municipality. Decree No. 14-19. Tbilisi.

[14]   Tbilisi City Assembly. 2019. The Land Use Master Plan of the Capital City. Decree No. 18-39 and Tbilisi City Assembly. 2016. Regulations on the Usage and Development of Territories in Tbilisi Municipality. Decree No. 14-19.

These wrong calculations of FAR and relevant areas are frequently the reason for too high density and other related problems. It is important to ensure the logical connection between legal zoning conditions and the factual physical environment. This sort of clarity on spatial–territorial and legal issues will balance the development and simplify the land management issues in the future. Figure 4.3 illustrates the difference given by the wrong interpretation of these guidelines.

In Figure 4.3 one can clearly see that the shared neighborhood street network is included in the land plots for the residential buildings. This way, the maximum FAR according to the land use master plan is used, net and gross FAR are almost equal, and the clear urban structure is not created. This sort of design also leads to difficulties in the future management of the site.

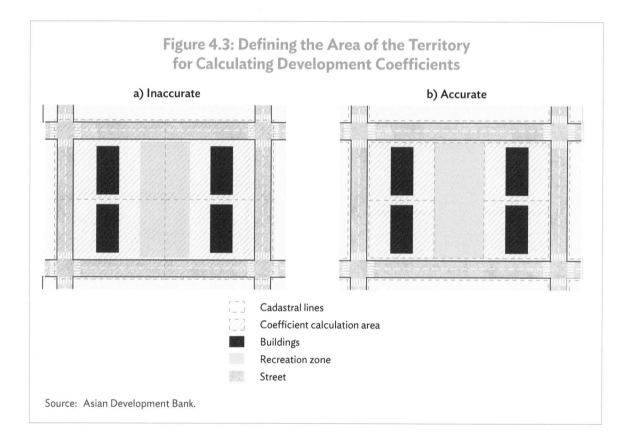

Figure 4.3: Defining the Area of the Territory for Calculating Development Coefficients

a) Inaccurate   b) Accurate

Cadastral lines
Coefficient calculation area
Buildings
Recreation zone
Street

Source: Asian Development Bank.

4.1.1.2 Population and Residential Density and/or Number

Population and residential density/number (person/ha, dwelling units/ha) is crucial in the development of a healthy residential environment.

There are no clear maximum or minimum allowed indicators for population and dwelling unit density in Georgia. Some guidelines are provided by the national legislation.[15]

---

[15] Government of Georgia. 2019. On the Rules for Developing Spatial and City Planning Documentation. Decree No. 260.

As per both documents, the gross population density should not exceed 300 persons/ha for multi-unit residential developments in seismic rayons.

According to UN-Habitat, the minimum density of population should be 150 persons/ha to ensure optimal development density, as well as to ensure sustainable urban development; however, it does not indicate a maximum number (footnote 12).

In the process of developing these guidelines, an urban analysis was conducted in Vake, one of the most densely populated districts of Tbilisi. Out of the identified 91 blocks, only 11 exceeded the density (of population) indicator of 300 persons/ha. Excessive density was identified in relatively new blocks that have not been developed with full consideration of the standards (Figure 4.4). The analysis confirms that it is possible to use these standards in practice and that they can be regarded as the maximum indicator for the density of population in Tbilisi.

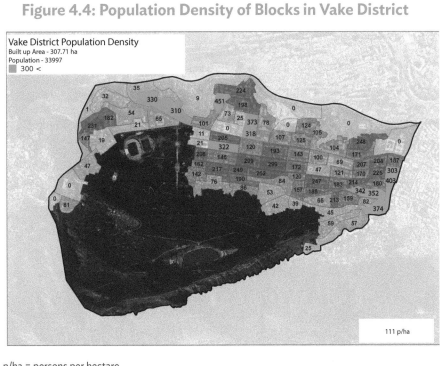

Figure 4.4: Population Density of Blocks in Vake District

ha = hectare, p/ha = persons per hectare.
Sources: Tbilisi City Hall and Asian Development Bank.

However, when discussing planning solutions, without more specific methodological guidelines for the calculation of the population and dwelling unit density/number, it is difficult to use the standard in practice. In the process of planning, questions arise as to how to define the maximum number of potential residents and dwelling units considering the construction area of the planned development and how many square meters of residential space should be considered per resident.

The safety technical regulations for buildings is recommended to be used as guidance to define the predicted population and dwelling units' density/number when discussing planning solutions.[16] In these regulations, an area of 18.6 square meters (m^2) is allocated for each occupant as residential space.[17] Based on this indicator a methodology for calculating the population and dwelling unit's gross density/number can be defined.

To define the maximum gross density of population in the residential area, the net residential area of the planned and/or existing buildings is first defined. As a rule, this makes up 75%–80% of the residential gross floor area used in the calculation of FAR.[18] A further 20%–25% is taken up by shared spaces such as halls, stairways, etc.[19] By dividing the final residential net floor area by 18.6 m^2, the maximum number of population that can live comfortably in the area can be calculated. If this number is divided by the total area (in hectares) of the territory, the gross density of the population (person/ha) is obtained (Box 4.3 and Figure 4.5).

Box 4.3: Sample Formula for Gross Population Density

Total residential area (m^2) x 0.75 (or 0.8) = net residential area (m^2)
Net residential area (m^2) / 18.6 m^2 = max residents (persons)
Max residents (persons) / total project area (ha) = gross density of population (person/ha)

Source: Authors.

When the exact number and area of dwelling units are not predefined, the following method can be used to calculate the density of dwelling units:

(i)   Define the average area of a dwelling unit. In this case, the average number of household members in Tbilisi is 3.3.[20]
(ii)   Multiply this by 18.6 m^2. The result is approximately 60 m^2 and can be regarded as the average area of a dwelling unit.

---

16   Government of Georgia. 2016. Technical Rules for the Safety of Constructions and Buildings. Decree No 41.
17   It is important to note that the 1989 SNIPs had set the minimum net residential area per person to 18 m^2.
18   In the old Soviet Union residential buildings.
19   idem.
20   Government of Georgia, National Statistics Office. General Population Census of 2014.

(iii) By dividing the net residential area by the average area of a dwelling unit on the planning territory, the probable number of dwelling units can be calculated.

(iv) Divide the total number of dwelling units by the total territory (in hectares) to calculate the approximate planned density of dwelling units (dwelling unit/ha) (Figure 4.5).

Figure 4.5: Methodology for Calculating Population and Residential Density/Number

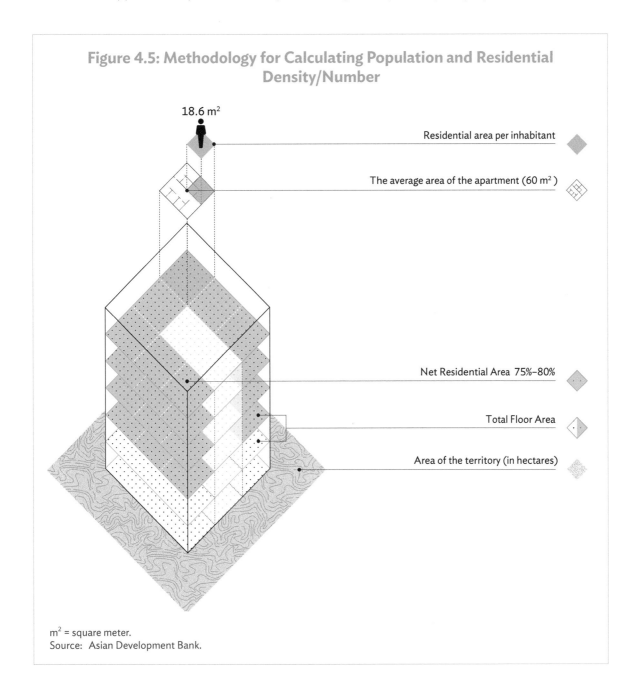

18.6 m²

Residential area per inhabitant

The average area of the apartment (60 m²)

Net Residential Area 75%–80%

Total Floor Area

Area of the territory (in hectares)

m² = square meter.
Source: Asian Development Bank.

4.2 Urban Structure and Requirements for Building Arrangements

In a dense development area, urban morphology as a whole, building typology, and the arrangement of the buildings are important factors that ensure a living environment of a high quality and fair chances of usability for different groups.

Urban structure is defined by various elements: street network, blocks, land plots, buildings, and open and green spaces (Figure 4.6). A careful arrangement of these elements creates a compact but well-balanced neighborhood of building structures and usable open spaces. Various types of urban morphology with spatial–compositional arrangement of these elements are possible with the same FAR (Figure 4.7).

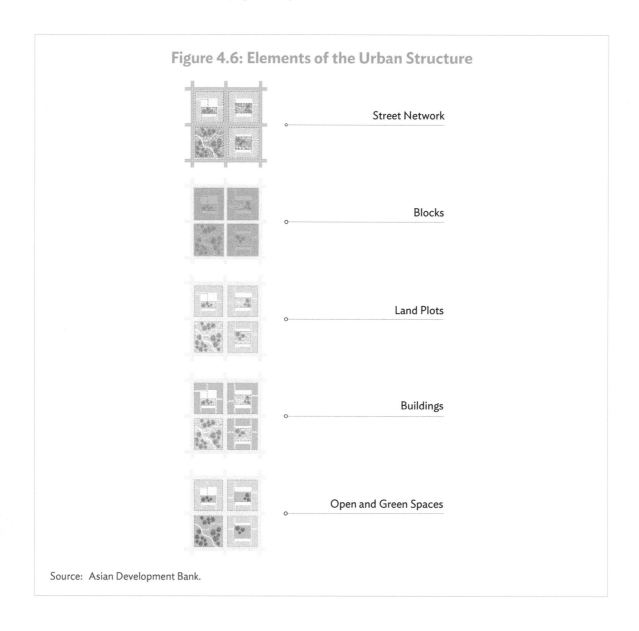

Figure 4.6: Elements of the Urban Structure

Street Network

Blocks

Land Plots

Buildings

Open and Green Spaces

Source: Asian Development Bank.

Figure 4.7: Different Types of Development with the Same Floor Area Ratio

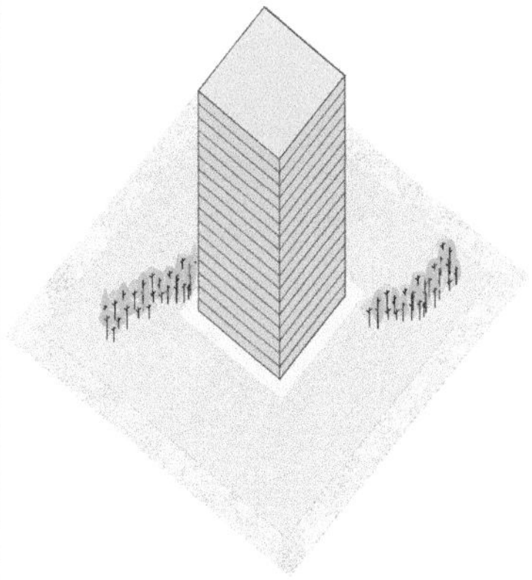

Block structure with multistory building typology

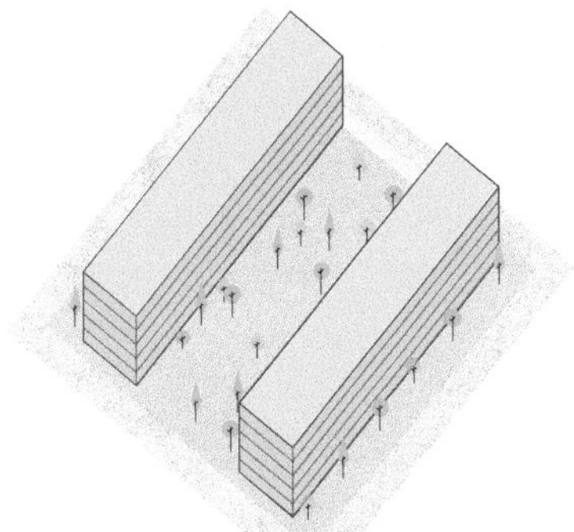

Block structure with linear building typology

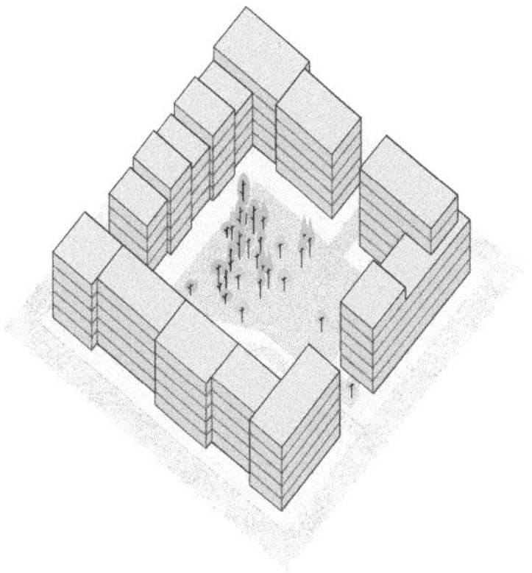

Semi-open perimeter block

Source: Asian Development Bank.

4.2.1 Street Network and Blocks

The street network and blocks are the main elements of urban morphology. Streets serve as a basis for urban development and form blocks, the major planning units. Blocks may significantly differ according to the street network configuration, topography, types and arrangement of buildings, as well as the distribution of plot lands.[21]

The possible arrangement of the street network and the block structure mainly depend on the location of the project area and on whether the area is already built-up. If the development takes place in built-up surroundings with existing access routes, the possibilities for the development are more limited. In this case, the existing street network clearly defines the block structure.

In the development of smaller brownfields or former industrial districts, the surrounding urban morphology and street network also have to be considered.

When integrating a planning area into an existing development structure, there should be good cohesion with the adjacent structures to avoid functional and physical isolation of new neighborhoods. To achieve this goal, cut-through and intersecting streets also have to be designed.

---

21 Urban Design Alliance. 2007. *Urban Design Compendium*. London: English Partnerships and The Housing Corporation. p. 62. https://webapps.stoke.gov.uk/uploadedfiles/Urban%20Design%20Compendium%201.pdf.

In unbuilt, formerly agricultural land with only one owner (or owners joined together in a development agency), the development is less dependent on external factors and urban design can be done more freely, as the streets can follow the envisioned building structures and optimal block layouts.

Many planners prefer standard-size blocks developed within a regular grid. Such configuration is characterized by a high street density and ensures high flexibility for pedestrians. Long blocks and buildings create barriers for pedestrians, whereas short blocks provide direct and short connections.

In Vienna, the maximum length and width of blocks is recommended not to exceed 150 meters (footnote 2). In Tbilisi, such blocks are encountered in the historic areas, in the Sololaki and Mtastminda neighborhoods (Figure 4.8).

Figure 4.8: Block Dimensions in the Sololaki Neighborhood

Source: Tbilisi City Hall.

Therefore, to form a mixed-use neighborhood with a lot of activities that is well integrated with surrounding areas and makes walking easier and safer, it is highly recommended to plan short, closed, or semi-open perimeter blocks.

Why perimeter blocks and not, for example, blocks with stand-alone (individual) high-rise buildings or linear buildings? To answer this question, it is sufficient to conduct a general comparative assessment of the positive and negative aspects of each (Figure 4.7).

In case of a closed or semi-open perimeter block, a clearly defined street network is formed. The inner side of the block is better protected from the street noise. Frequent and intensive mixed uses, such as grocery shops, offices, and small dentist clinics on the ground floor level along the main streets contribute to a vivid street life and raises the attractiveness of the public space. The streets that are busy and active most of the time during the day provide safety for walking. Such functional diversity in the public space supports social control and increases the sense of safety. In case of a perimeter block, a semi-public inner yard can be created within the block, which is distinguished by the sense of safety and territorial belonging. Compared to other development typology, perimeter blocks can provide the same gross floor area with a better human scale, where the height of the buildings is lower (Example 3).[22]

Example 3

Semi-open perimeter block in Vake district. Case study area in between Arakishvili, Paliashvili, Abashidze, and Rigi streets as good example from Tbilisi's built environment (photo by Tbilisi City Hall).

---

22   If the floor numbers are higher than recommended, then perimeter block development will lose its human scale and all its good qualities altogether.

In the case of linear buildings, similar to perimeter blocks, a clearly defined street network is formed that supports a mix of uses located on the ground floors along main streets. The inner buildings are protected from street noise; however, the risk of alleviated noise among the buildings due to the narrower dimension of the open spaces between the buildings increases. The linear open spaces left between the buildings have a reduced functionality. For example, it is not recommended to build a sports field between buildings that are close to each other due to the high level of noise from the field. In contrast to perimeter blocks, open and green spaces are more fragmented and children and the elderly feel less secure and safe in them (Example 4).

Example 4

Linear buildings. An example of linear buildings from Tbilisi, Vaja-pshavela, sixth block (photo by Tbilisi City Hall).

In case of blocks planned with stand-alone high-rise buildings, the number of corner dwelling units with good lighting and two-way ventilation is higher. In addition, the highest floors have quite nice views. However, at the same time, they generally do not contribute to a functionally diverse urban environment and an active street network cannot be developed since high-rise buildings are developed only in certain spots. This typology also creates open spaces that are not protected from strong winds and street noise, makes social control challenging to implement (section 4.2.3), and reduces the sense of territorial belonging due to the reduction of the human scale (Example 5).[23]

---

23   Alexander, C. et al. 2010. *A Pattern Language: Towns, Buildings, Construction.* New York: Oxford University Press. pp. 81; and J. Gehl. 2010. *Cities for People.* Washington, DC: Island Press.

Fair Shared City: Guidelines for Socially Inclusive and Gender-Responsive Residential Development

Stand-alone high-rise buildings. An example of stand-alone high-rise buildings in Tbilisi, Nutsubidze slope, 3rd Microrayon (photo by Tbilisi City Hall).

Working with the human scale means changing priorities in the planning process. It involves considering and assessing human physical abilities and restrictions. In the planning process, the following questions must be answered:

(i)   How do people perceive the environment around them?

(ii)   How do people move around?

(iii)   What is regarded to be safe and comfortable for people?

Work on organizing spaces and designing buildings only starts after this analysis has been completed. However, even when this process starts, the process needs to constantly return to the stage of assessing human scale.

In Tbilisi, on Dirsi planning territory (second stage), the process of drawing up a plan for the development regulation took into account the guidelines of the agency in building the development structure.[24] As a result, a quiet, safe, and interconnected urban structure was designed (Figure 4.9).

---

[24]   Some recommendations were provided during the meetings at the Tbilisi City Hall. The rest of the recommendations can be found in the letter of former Tbilisi Municipality Urban Development Department (letter N:201919857).

Figure 4.9: Dirsi Residential Complex, Second Stage

a) Fragment of the Project

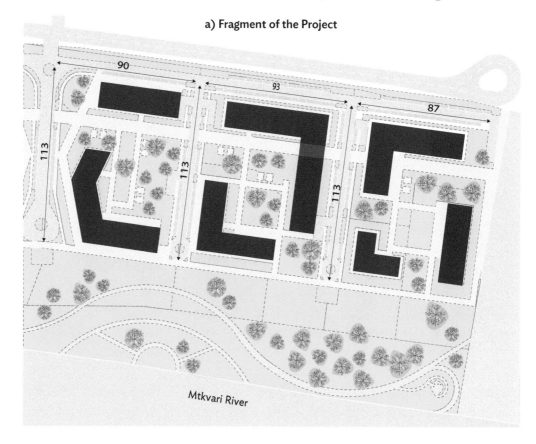

Mtkvari River

b) 3D Visualization of the Fragment from the Project

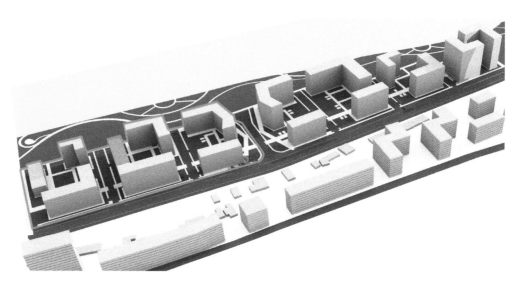

Source: Resolution N413-2019, 20.12.2019. Tbilisi City Assembly; edited by ADB.

One of the major objectives of planning is to create walkable neighborhoods where the street network is interconnected and avoids dead ends. Topography and terrain slope have to be considered in the planning process. In areas that have steep slopes, it can be more difficult to develop a regular grid, but the goal should still be to create as much interconnectivity as possible to enable comfortable walking. Even in this case, it is still possible to plan a twisted block system and for more connectivity, additional pedestrian pathways (Figure 4.10).

Figure 4.10: Irregular Grid Structure Examples from Tbilisi Neighborhoods

a) Upper Sololaki Neighborhood

b) Nadzaladevi Neighborhood

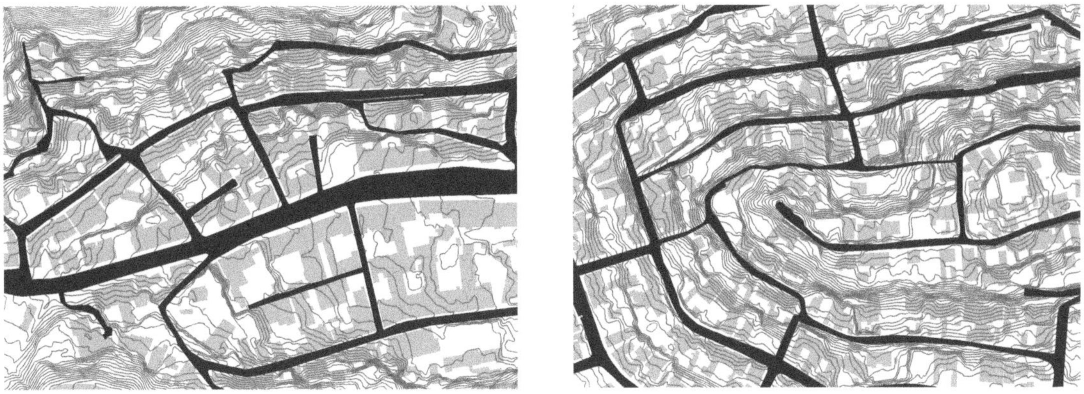

Sources: Tbilisi Transport and Urban Development Agency and ADB.

In case interconnected streets cannot be formed and dead ends have to be designed, the maximum length of each dead end should not exceed 150 meters (m). A dead-end with a length of over 50 m should have a square at the end where a fire truck can turn around. The dimensions of the square should be at least 15 x 15 m.[25]

The access paths to residential houses should be safe, well-lit, and barrier-free. Barriers can be visual like high concrete fences, or physical like slopes and different levels of surfaces, stairs, but also long ways, etc. For comfortable walking, it is also recommended to limit vehicle movement to the highest possible degree within inner areas of residential compounds or joint spaces with no strict distinction between spaces designated for vehicles and pedestrians.

The space for pedestrians along the district or neighborhood roads should comply at least with minimal standards. In particular, a path or a sidewalk for pedestrians planned within a residential development is recommended to be at least 2.5 m along the driving road (footnote 15).

---

25 Government of Georgia. State Sub-Department of the Ministry of Internal Affairs to Emergency Management Service. 22 February 2021 (Letter MIA 7 21 00428069).

Car garage entrances and driveways to parking lots should be avoided along busy streets to prevent barriers to public transportation and active pedestrian movement. If possible, alternative access routes from backyards or parallel streets for commercial site visitors and distribution services should be offered.

4.2.2 Land Plots

A development area or even single blocks have to be divided into land plots. Land plots must be based on the logic of spatial–territorial planning. There should be a clear distinction between net areas for residential and non-residential buildings and areas for common spaces, such as streets and other open spaces. Each area should later be defined by the relevant functional zone. This principle of spatial–territorial planning is important for developing a fair shared living environment, where issues of territorial belonging and its future management are clearly defined. Areas developed without adhering to the noted principle often appear confusing to visitors. Their further development into a well-functioning neighborhood is proven to be difficult.

In the process of urban development in Tbilisi, the fragmented residential districts represent an important challenge. Due to the inordinate registration of land plots, developments do not follow the spatial planning logic. This is confirmed by examples from various neighborhoods in Tbilisi (Boxes 4.4 and 4.5).

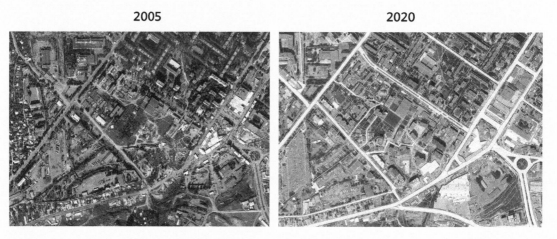

Box 4.4: An Example of Chaotic Development from the Gldani District

2005 **2020**

The development between Khizabavri, Sheshelidze, Kerchi, and Vasadze streets in Gldani district did not follow the spatial planning logic. Once undeveloped territory was divided into land plots and registered without any spatial logic. Over time, each land plot developed independently and in a fragmented manner without any meaningful change in the spatial organization of land plots. Such isolated "islands" lead to fragmented residential development without consideration of everyday life quality, as there is no distinguished street network or attractive and usable public or recreational spaces of adequate size.

Source: Tbilisi Transport and Urban Development Agency.

When land plots are registered without consideration of the surrounding plots, it is recommended to use land readjustment as a planning tool. Land readjustment allows for the reorganization of land plots in the development area. As a result, the space for the street network, engineering infrastructure, social infrastructure, and public spaces is allocated. The rest of the territory is divided among landowners accordingly. If necessary, landowners are asked to give up some percentage of their property. In this case, the landowners' property size is reduced but the value of the land is increased. Land readjustment allows municipalities to provide basic infrastructure and public spaces for the future neighborhood. This approach is beneficial for both the private and the public sectors. The private sector benefits from increased land value and better conditions for approval of city planning documentation and construction permits based on well-organized land plots (Figure 4.11).

In dense urban environments, the area and proportion of land plots should not be inadequately small or large. In case there are large (areas and dimensions) plots, territories develop mono-functionally. Often, such territories have monotonous architecture and massive residential buildings. Dividing a territory into many land plots supports the development of architectural and functional diversity. The space is rationally utilized and there are no unused areas. However, in case there are a bigger number of small size land plots, the construction of buildings requires much more capital. This is why it is difficult to develop affordable housing. Therefore, it is necessary to strike some kind of a balance between the two approaches. For example, development can proceed with larger land plots with the goal of forming an affordable residential fund. In this case, the effect of diversity should be achieved through different architectural solutions (Boxes 4.6 and 4.7).

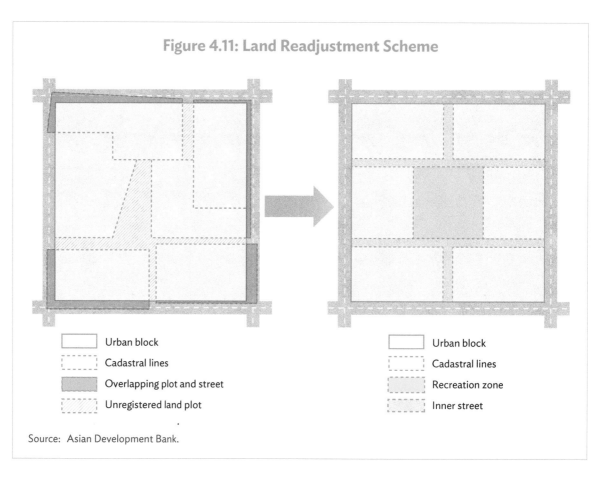

Figure 4.11: Land Readjustment Scheme

	Urban block
	Cadastral lines
	Overlapping plot and street
	Unregistered land plot

	Urban block
	Cadastral lines
	Recreation zone
	Inner street

Source: Asian Development Bank.

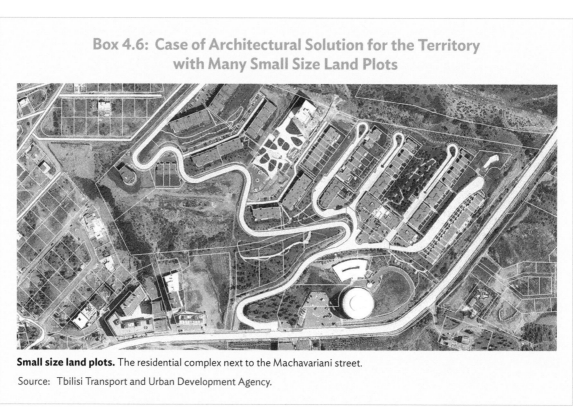

Box 4.6: Case of Architectural Solution for the Territory with Many Small Size Land Plots

Small size land plots. The residential complex next to the Machavariani street.

Source: Tbilisi Transport and Urban Development Agency.

Large land plots. Dirsi residential complex (first phase).

Source: Tbilisi Transport and Urban Development Agency.

When planning a dense residential development, it is recommended that the front length of each land plot (land width) is shorter than the plot depth. In addition, the front length of each plot of land should not be less than 15–20 m wide and 25 m deep (footnote 15).

4.2.3 Building Structures and Proportions

In planning, ensuring sufficient natural light inside dwellings depends on the arrangement of buildings on land plots. In case of an eastern–western orientation of the building, the depth of the building is recommended to be 15 m, while a northern–southern orientation has to have a depth of 12 m to ensure sufficient sunlight within the dwelling units (footnote 2). These building widths allow dwelling units to extend through the whole wing-depth, so they are well-lit in every part and ensure two-way ventilation and partial protection from the street noise. The quality of these dwelling units is much higher than the quality of one-side oriented units in deep wing buildings.

Visual contact and audibility between dwelling units and open space are restricted by increasing building height. It is recommended not to exceed five or six floors beyond which sensory perception is already markedly impaired.[26] This is a factor of special importance for persons with childcare duties or elderly persons, as the possibility of such contacts enables them to watch their children playing outside or to have a share in everyday life in the street or courtyard from the window.

Sensory perception between buildings and open spaces. Case study perimeter block from Vake District (Photo by Gvantsa Nikolaishvili/ADB).

For the impression of a human scale, this "border" of five or six floors also proves important. It should be noted that buildings with more than five or six floors create a greater sense of alienation in the neighborhood.

If floor numbers are higher, then it is recommended not to exceed seven or eight floors and proper attention should be paid toward designing open spaces (section 4.5). Recessed roof floors can help.

---

26   In case of the sixth floor, it should be a setback.

4.2.4 Analysis of Movement of the Sun and Shading

Sufficient sunlight and shading are among the central criteria for assessing the quality of urban design and its impacts. On the basis of the analysis of shading, we can assess the impact of the height and the spatial planning arrangement of the building structure, and for adjacent structures on the planning territory. In case of a poorly designed high-density development, it is highly possible that open spaces will not have sufficient sunlight.

The assessment of shading and sunlight takes place in spring and autumn. The analysis is conducted on the basis of observation on 1 April and 1 October (at the following times: 9:00 a.m., 11:00 a.m., 1:00 p.m., 3:00 p.m., and 5:00 p.m.).

An open space is considered well-lit if at least one-third, but better if 40% has sunlight at 11:00 a.m. or 3:00 p.m (footnote 2). In addition, children's playgrounds and benches should be placed in the sunny spots and shading facilities should be considered for hot summer periods (Figure 4.12).

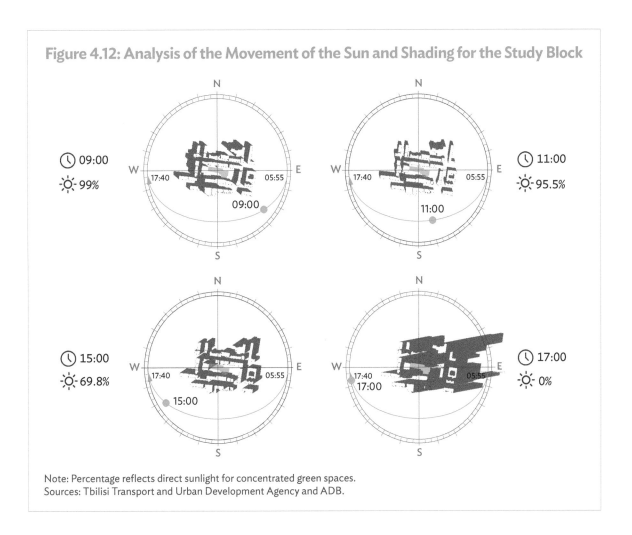

Figure 4.12: Analysis of the Movement of the Sun and Shading for the Study Block

09:00
99%

11:00
95.5%

15:00
69.8%

17:00
0%

Note: Percentage reflects direct sunlight for concentrated green spaces.
Sources: Tbilisi Transport and Urban Development Agency and ADB.

A simple configuration of concentrated green spaces eases their functioning and usage. The proportion of building height to the width of the concentrated green space should be at least 1:2 to avoid excessive shading effects, a sense of cramped feeling of space among users, and conflict between various functional usages.[27]

A planning dilemma is that users highly appreciate sunlight in spring and in autumn whereas in hot summer periods, lack of shade becomes a problem. In regard to this season cycle, trees are the best natural shading elements, as they provide maximum shade in summer and let more sunlight through in other seasons.

4.2.5 Sight Axes and Landmarks

The spatial–compositional arrangement should consider spatial axes and landmarks identified in a particular district or neighborhood. The spatial and visual balance in a residential district or neighborhood should not be compromised by a planning proposal (Box 4.8).

Box 4.8: An Illustration of Spatial Axes and a Landmark as a Result of Unbalanced Development

1970   2021

Before and after. The Archives Building at the corner of Pekini and Vazha-Pshavela Avenues (left photo from the Georgian national archive; right photo from Tbilisi City Hall).

---

27   The Study Städtebauliche Kennwerte, MA 18- Urban Development Planning, Vienna 2017. p. 254. https://www.raumumwelt. at/wp-content/uploads/2018/11/7_1_3_Werkstattbericht167_Downloadversion_klein.pdf.

When the development only includes one side of the street in existing surroundings, the height and dimensions of buildings on the other street side should be taken into consideration when designing new buildings. In case of high density, transitions to existing structures should be gradual. It is recommended that buildings of the same height are built on both sides of the street, retaining the scale and a holistic perception of the street. In this case, high-rise buildings should not be placed on the street front.

4.2.6 Architectural and Design Elements

To ensure safety and comfort and to reduce the risk of violence or harassment, building entrances and hallways should be free of barriers, as well as visible and well-lit. Stairs and corridors are recommended to have natural lighting. In addition, corridors or arches should be designed as cut-through so that they connect the building to internal and external spaces of the block through the shortest paths possible.

To ensure safety, artificial barriers such as high and long concrete fences should be replaced with small architectural elements, greenery, and urban furniture. It is important to have social control along the spaces designated for pedestrians and it is also important that pedestrians do not have a feeling of being alarmed and locked in when walking around and that they can physically escape in case of need (Example 6).

Example 6

Artificial barrier. Artificial barrier next to the former Hippodrome creating a locked walkway (photo by Gvantsa Nikolaishvili/ADB).

4.3 Social Infrastructure and Accessibility

A city of short distances implies the formation of neighborhoods where social infrastructure is located within walking distance. People have to go to many places during the day when carrying out unpaid work. For example, when taking a child to a school and/or kindergarten, buying groceries, taking children for a walk in a park, etc. Long blocks between destinations increase the distance one has to cover and allow less flexibility of movement or traveling around. A development structure with short blocks and a frequent and intensive street network should be a precondition.

Social infrastructure is defined as the facilities that provide various social services needed on a daily basis (such as education, health care, culture, civic safety, sports, religious and/or spiritual, housing, etc.) and are located in walking distance (footnote 14). In a dense urban structure, the existence of basic functions for various groups in walking distance decreases the level of car dependency and supports diverse and mixed-use development in the district or neighborhood. If such functions are situated near homes, this makes everyday life easier for elderly citizens, children, parents, and other persons involved in care work (Box 4.9).

Box 4.9: Negative Consequences of Pedestrian Accessibility Deficit of Social Infrastructure in the Neighborhood

Some parents live in a peripheral district or neighborhood but work in the city center and take their child or children to a kindergarten in a different district or neighborhood. They experience fatigue as well as constant stress from traveling long distances. This situation is true for citizens in districts or neighborhoods with a shortage of kindergartens, or where the resources of existing kindergartens have been exhausted. The same is true for other types of social infrastructure as well, for example, schools and green facilities such as playgrounds and parks. Such functional disconnection and territorial fragmentation in everyday life hinders children's socialization in the neighborhood as well as formation of good neighborhood relations or a sense of community. This also applies to adults. Such social networks are the "social capital" of a residential area and have a specific high importance for groups of the population, which have a high local orientation and strongly relate to the quality of their living environment.

Source: Asian Development Bank.

As a rule, an adult has a walking speed of 5 to 6 kilometers per hour (kph). This means that an adult can cover approximately 500 m in 5 to 6 minutes and approximately 1 kilometer (km) in 10 minutes. In addition, 500 m are regarded as the desirable maximum distance for walking for an adult to buy groceries or take children to school. If the daily life infrastructure is further away, people are inclined to use cars, cumulatively leading to problems of transportation congestion in the city. These figures are reduced by almost half in the case of elderly people. The optimal time to get to their desired destination in their case is regarded to be 5 to 6 minutes. They can cover around 250 m in 6 minutes. In general, they need access to pharmacies and doctors' offices more often (Figure 4.13).

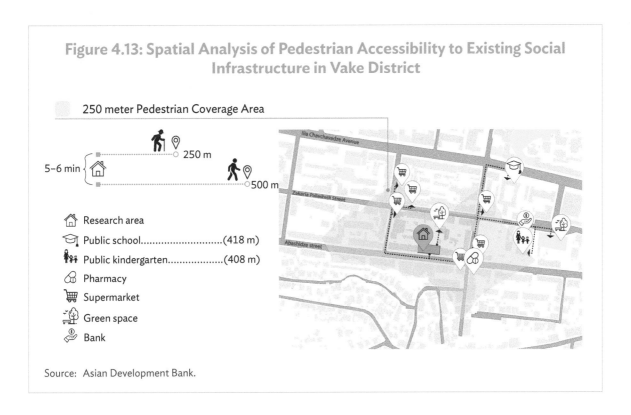

Figure 4.13: Spatial Analysis of Pedestrian Accessibility to Existing Social Infrastructure in Vake District

250 meter Pedestrian Coverage Area

5–6 min
250 m
500 m

⌂ Research area
🎓 Public school............................(418 m)
👪 Public kindergarten...................(408 m)
⚕ Pharmacy
🛒 Supermarket
🌳 Green space
💰 Bank

Ilia Chavchavadze Avenue
Zakaria Paliashvili Street
Abashidze street

Source: Asian Development Bank.

When designing social infrastructure, in addition to considering the catchment areas, it is important to ensure safe and barrier-free walking paths to key sites, enabling the whole population, especially the elderly, children, and caretakers, to move around independently and comfortably, including with prams, wheelchairs, or rollators (Box 4.10).

Box 4.10: Illustrations of Noninclusive Pedestrian Crossings

Noninclusive pedestrian crossings. Next to former hippodrome area (photo by Gvantsa Nikolaishvili/ADB).

continued on next page

Planning Criteria and Methodological Guidelines

Box 4.10 *continued*

Noninclusive pedestrian crossings. On Marshal Archil Gelovani avenue (photo by Gvantsa Nikolaishvili/ADB).

4.4 Public Kindergartens and Schools

High-quality kindergartens and schools with sufficient capacity are especially important in the development of compact, sustainable, and comfortable residential neighborhoods or districts.

However, in parallel with the fast pace of urbanization in Tbilisi, the demand on social infrastructure increases. Empirical evidence shows that the existing infrastructure is overcrowded and exhausted and many districts or neighborhoods experience a deficit. In addition, it is difficult to find territories to build new kindergartens and schools to cope with this deficit. Meeting territorial requirements envisaged by legislation in dense urban developments such as Tbilisi is a challenge for both the municipality and the private sector. As a result, Tbilisi has many kindergartens with insufficient open and green spaces.

Therefore, when planning new residential neighborhoods or districts, it is important to respond to these challenges. These guidelines present simplified recommendations in contrast to the existing national legislation.

Building any new residential complex creates a cohort of additional kindergarten and school-age children in the near future. Therefore, there is increased burden on the capacity of the existing infrastructure or the issue of building new infrastructure becomes a topic for discussion. The municipality and the Ministry of Education, Science, Culture and Sports are obliged to develop public infrastructure for new cohorts of pupils. In order to do this, they need information on the prospective number of kindergarten and school-age children to calculate the necessary infrastructure and space area.

To establish the prospective number of kindergarten and school-age children, the data from the National Statistics Agency of Georgia can be used. Based on data from the 2014 census, the percentage of kindergarten children (2–6 years) in the total population of Tbilisi is approximately 5.9% and the percentage of school-age children (6–19 years) is approximately 15.3%.[28]

Based on these indicators, the approximate prospective number of school-age and kindergarten children in the project area can be established. After assessing the capacity of existing social infrastructure adjacent to the planning territory, the need for building new infrastructure can be identified.

If social infrastructure in a residential neighborhood or district is overcrowded or the planning solution envisages settlement of 400–600 and more school children, it is recommended to designate a space to build a public school within the planning area. When defining the area of school territories, the existing national legislation[29] envisages the usage of "SNIP."[30]

Based on these norms, schools can be divided into several categories according to their capacity and territory allocated per child (Table 4.1).

For schools with more than 1,000 students, several individual buildings have to be planned (for example, in the newly built school N 186 in Dighomi). It is recommended for schools to have three floors; however, for dense developments, four floors could also be planned (footnote 30).

Table 4.1: Categories of Schools According to Existing National Regulations in Georgia

School Territory	Number of Children	Area of Project Territory Per Child (m^2/child)
Small school	400–600	50
Mid-size school	600–800	40
Large school	800–1,100	33
Mega school	1,100–2,000 and more	21

m^2 = square meter.
Source: On the approval of arrangement, equipment and sanitary rules and norms of pre-school and general education institutions. Order No. 308. Government of Georgia, Ministry of Labor, Health and Social Affairs. 2001.

---

28 Government of Georgia, National Statistics Office. 2 December 2020 (Letter N9-2740).
29 Government of Georgia, Ministry of Labor, Health and Social Affairs. 2001. Order No. 308: On the Approval of Arrangement, Equipment and Sanitary Rules and Norms of Pre-School and General Education Institutions.
30 SNIP in 1991 publication published by Committee of Architecture and Urban Planning of the Republic of Georgia.

Considering limited municipal land resources and urban context in the capital, it is recommended to reduce the territory allocated per child by 40%.[31] For example, to build a school with a capacity of 400 children, for the planning territory, the indicator of 50 m^2/child should be reduced to 30 m^2/child in Tbilisi. A school with a capacity of 600 children can reduce the area allotted per child to 24 m^2 from 40 m^2. The Ministry of Education, Science, Culture and Sports will discuss the issue of building a public school on the identified territory.[32]

In addition, considering that there is a shortage of municipal land to build public schools in the city, it is recommended to give preference to schools with a capacity of 600 or more students. Doing so will make it possible to better use the allocated territory to accommodate more children in the neighborhood.

The national legislation recognizes two types of kindergartens. The first type is an individual two-story building that can be built with a minimum capacity for 140 children. The second type of kindergarten can be attached to a residential building with a capacity of not more than 140 children. In both cases, the area of the territory for the kindergarten should be calculated as 35 m^2/child (footnote 30).

However, as was already noted, considering the urban context of Tbilisi, it is quite difficult to comply with these regulations in a dense development. Considering this, it is recommended to arrange integrated kindergartens on the ground floors of multi-apartment residential buildings with a dedicated entrance and independent open spaces. Such practice is encountered in the city of Vienna as well (for example, in the Querbet social housing) (Figure 4.14).[33] In case a municipal kindergarten is integrated into a multi-apartment residential building, its capacity should not be less than 140 children (in a development planned for about 2,300 inhabitants, i.e., 700 dwelling units on average). If a kindergarten is integrated on the ground floor of a multi-apartment residential building, it is also necessary to build a fenced yard with sufficient area.

---

31   Government of Georgia, Ministry of Education, Science, Culture and Sports. 22 March 2021 (Letter MES 8 21 0000267131).
32   Government of Georgia, Ministry of Education, Science, Culture and Sports. 4 November 2020 (Letter MES 1 20 0001066371).
33   ArchDaily. 2021. Querbeet Social Housing / Synn Architekten. https://www.archdaily.com/934266/querbeet-social-housing-synn-architekten-zt-og.

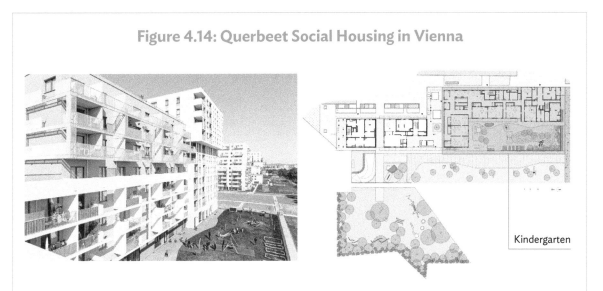

Figure 4.14: Querbeet Social Housing in Vienna

Kindergarten

Source: ArchDaily. 2021. Querbeet Social Housing / Synn Architekten. https://www.archdaily.com/934266/querbeet-social-housing-synn-architekten-zt-og.

A separate playground for each group should be included on the land plot as per the established norms: for children 2–5 years of age there should be a playground with 7.5 m^2/child, for children 5–6 years of age, it should be 7.5 m^2/child (footnote 30). If there is no information about the age group of children, it is recommended to consider 7.5 m^2/child. Thus, a kindergarten for 140 children will have a yard with an area of at least 1,000 m^2.

It is recommended to build kindergartens and schools in the depth of a microrayon or a block far away from industrial sites, streets with intensive traffic, and highways. When planning buildings for schools and kindergartens, each building should be placed separately on an isolated land plot. The catchment area should not exceed 300 m for kindergartens and 750 m for schools (footnote 14). Walking access to an educational institution should be safe and barrier-free. For example, children should not have to use or cross highways or streets with no safe sidewalks or pedestrian crosswalks. See Figure 4.15 for the example of the spatial analysis of accessibility to schools and kindergartens in Vake District.

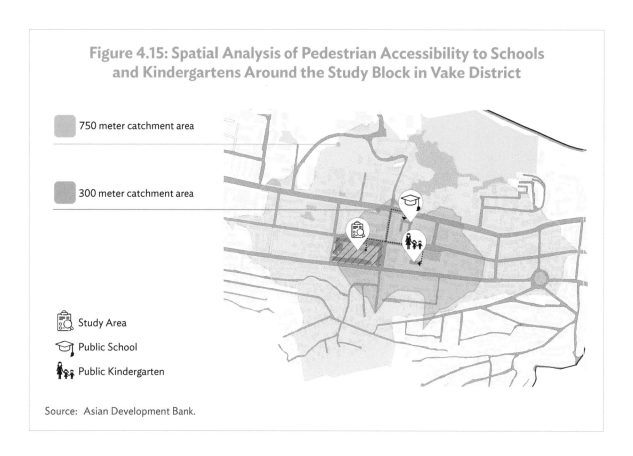

Figure 4.15: Spatial Analysis of Pedestrian Accessibility to Schools and Kindergartens Around the Study Block in Vake District

750 meter catchment area

300 meter catchment area

Study Area

Public School

Public Kindergarten

Source: Asian Development Bank.

4.5 Green Spaces

This section should be read alongside *Fair Shared Green and Recreational Spaces: Guidelines for Gender-Responsive and Inclusive Design*.[34] These guidelines provide more detailed information on designing parks and recreation areas that are inclusive and gender-responsive.

Complying with the principles of a fair and green city means that accessible and high-quality open and green spaces are adapted to the needs of all social groups. Special attention is paid to their function, location, size, and quality. The larger the population in the district or neighborhood, the more recreational spaces need to be planned. It is important that the green spaces in the city (parks, yards, squares, and boulevards) create a unified and well-connected system.

It is necessary to develop parks, gardens, squares, and other open public spaces adapted to the needs of all social groups at an adequate walking distance across residential areas, neighborhoods, and microrayons. These areas should offer possibilities for various types of activities, such as playgrounds for different age groups, open spaces for youths, resting areas for the elderly, zones for walking dogs, etc.

---

34 ADB and Tbilisi City Hall. 2021. *Fair Shared Green and Recreational Spaces: Guidelines for Gender-Responsive and Inclusive Design*. Manila. https://www.adb.org/sites/default/files/publication/762081/green-spaces-guidelines-gender-responsive-design-tbilisi.pdf.

As per the Land Use Master Plan of Tbilisi, the area of green and open spaces designated for public usage should increase in the built up area of the city and exceed 10 m^2 per resident at the neighborhood level.[35] To comply with the requirements of the land use master plan and mitigate the deficit of green spaces in the capital and develop healthy residential neighborhoods, Table 4.2 presents recommended categories for shared green spaces on urban territories as well as the minimal spatial standards to follow.[36] It is recommended to consider the issue of ensuring neighborhood- and district-level green spaces when planning new project territories. In addition, the analysis conducted in Vake rayon demonstrated the deficit of neighborhood and district level green spaces, which hampers access to shared parks for a certain part of the population (Figure 4.16).

Table 4.2: Categories of Public Green Spaces According to Planning Level and Spatial Indicators

Categories	Pedestrian Catchment Area[a] (m)	Size of the Public Green Space[a] (ha)	Allocated Space per Inhabitant (m^2)
Local (Block)	250	0.16 –1.00[b]	3.5[c]
Neighborhood (Microrayon)	500	1.00–3.00	4.0[d]
Residential District	1,000	3.00–10.00	4.0[d]
	1,500	10.00–15.00	
City	2,000	> 15.00	>10.0[e]

ha = hectare, m = meter, m^2 = square meter.

[a] City of Vienna. 2017. Guidelines for determining the green area parameters as an auxiliary document for the green area plans (Leitfaden zur Ermittlung der Grünraum Kennwerte als Beitrag zum Lokalen Grünplan), MA 18-Urban Development and Planning. Construction norms and rules (SNIP), City Planning and Development of Urban and Rural Settlements, Committee of Architecture and Urban Planning of Georgian Republic, 2.07.01-89, p. 39-41. Tbilisi 1991.

[b] In the existing dense urban environment it is possible to design even smaller local parks.

[c] City of Vienna. 2013. Manual for Gender Mainstreaming in Urban Planning and Urban Development, MA 18 – Urban Development and Planning, p.35. https://www.wien.gv.at/stadtentwicklung/studien/pdf/b008358.pdf (accessed 21 May 2021).

[d] City of Vienna. 2017. Guidelines for determining the green area parameters as an auxiliary document for the green area plans (Leitfaden zur Ermittlung der Grünraum Kennwerte als Beitrag zum Lokalen Grünplan), MA 18 – Urban Development and Planning.

[e] Construction norms and rules (SNIP), City Planning and Development of Urban and Rural Settlements, Committee of Architecture and Urban Planning of Georgian Republic, 2.07.01-89, p. 38, Tbilisi 1991.

Note: Green spaces are parks, yards, squares, and boulevards.

Source: Asian Development Bank.

The area for green spaces on a particular project site is calculated in the planning process on the basis of the existing capacity of green spaces and its accessibility in a particular rayon, district, and neighborhood. The pre-planning process should identify whether there are public parks and squares near the project area. Based on the noted data, the existing resources of green spaces (public parks, gardens, squares) can be defined and whether or not it is necessary to plan a new public or semi-public green space within the project area can be determined.

---

[35]   The Land Use Master Plan of the Capital City. Decree No. 18–39. Tbilisi Municipality Assembly. 2019.

[36]   Due to the lack of the spatial data about green spaces in Tbilisi and the absence of the categorization of the green spaces it was really difficult to come up with a more detailed category system and indicators.

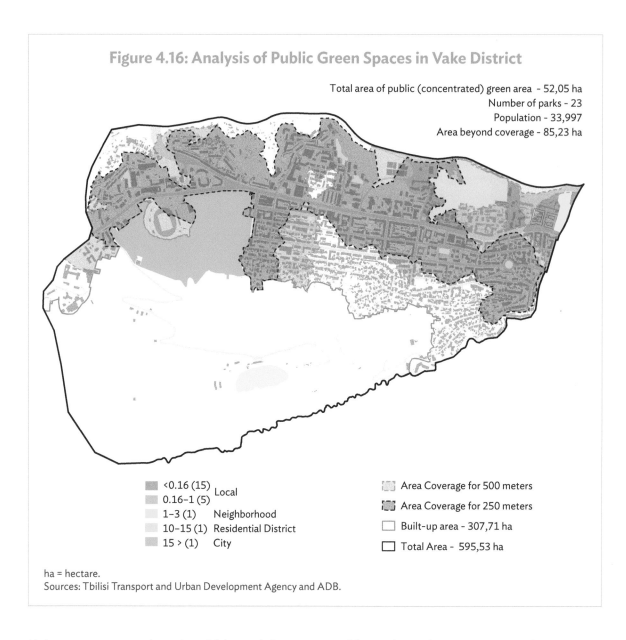

Figure 4.16: Analysis of Public Green Spaces in Vake District

Total area of public (concentrated) green area - 52,05 ha
Number of parks - 23
Population - 33,997
Area beyond coverage - 85,23 ha

<0.16 (15) Local	Area Coverage for 500 meters
0.16–1 (5)	Area Coverage for 250 meters
1–3 (1) Neighborhood	Built-up area - 307,71 ha
10–15 (1) Residential District	Total Area - 595,53 ha
15 > (1) City	

ha = hectare.
Sources: Tbilisi Transport and Urban Development Agency and ADB.

If the project area is less than 10 ha and there is no public park, garden, or square in the 250 m of pedestrian catchment area, the project site itself should include a public or semi-public concentrated green space. When designing such concentrated green areas, as per Table 4.2, it is recommended to consider 3.5 m^2 per inhabitant. A concentrated green space can include areas for resting, children's playgrounds, pedestrian pathways, and other spaces included in the greening plan. This does not include lawns along the streets, small green islands, and other similar areas. The depth of the semi-public or public green space should not be less than 25 m.

However, if the territory is more than 10 ha and there is no public park in 250 m of pedestrian catchment area, the project site should include a neighborhood level public or semi-public concentrated green space with 4 m^2 per inhabitant.[37] If there is a barrier-free and

---

[37]   The area bigger than 10 ha is already a different planning level (neighborhood/microrayon).

well-accessible public park at minimum within 250 m of catchment area, then there is no need to develop a new park on the project area.

In case these requirements cannot be met for neighborhood and district level green spaces, a minimum of 30% of the project area should be used for green spaces, out of which a minimum of 10% should be a concentrated and organized semi-public or public green space. To establish this criterion, data from the regulatory plans for several developments approved in Tbilisi within the last several years were assessed (Figure 4.17).

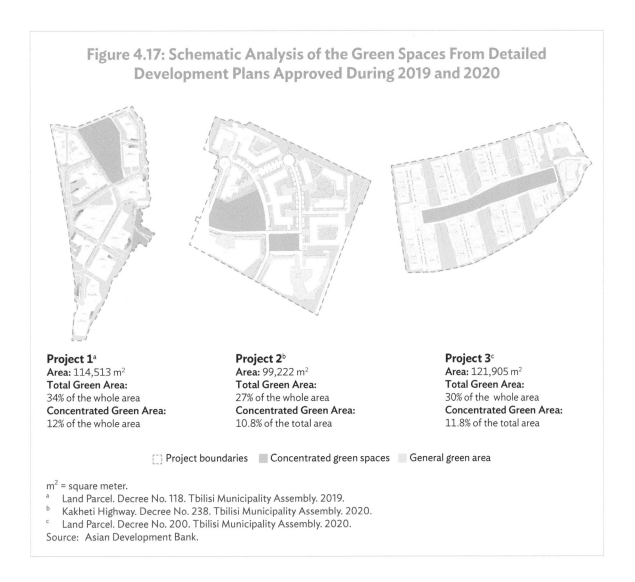

Figure 4.17: Schematic Analysis of the Green Spaces From Detailed Development Plans Approved During 2019 and 2020

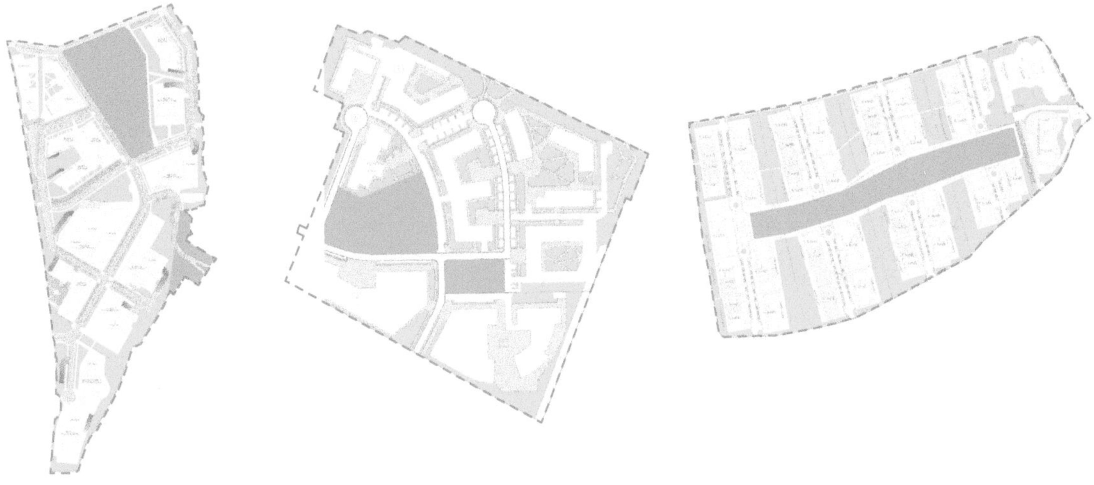

Project 1[a]
Area: 114,513 m^2
Total Green Area:
34% of the whole area
Concentrated Green Area:
12% of the whole area

Project 2[b]
Area: 99,222 m^2
Total Green Area:
27% of the whole area
Concentrated Green Area:
10.8% of the total area

Project 3[c]
Area: 121,905 m^2
Total Green Area:
30% of the whole area
Concentrated Green Area:
11.8% of the total area

Project boundaries | Concentrated green spaces | General green area

m^2 = square meter.
[a] Land Parcel. Decree No. 118. Tbilisi Municipality Assembly. 2019.
[b] Kakheti Highway. Decree No. 238. Tbilisi Municipality Assembly. 2020.
[c] Land Parcel. Decree No. 200. Tbilisi Municipality Assembly. 2020.
Source: Asian Development Bank.

One more effective criteria to assess whether the spatial balance within a block or a land plot within the project proposal is ensured is the area of the unbuilt territory, i.e., open space per inhabitant (Figure 4.18). This criterion is related to the density of the population and regulates sufficient open space allocation in the context of high density. Open spaces include green territories, pathways, roads, and open parking lots. At the initial stage of urban planning, an assessment of open spaces will provide an understanding of the planned development.

For a well-balanced urban morphology, 8 m^2 per inhabitant is recommended. When this indicator is adhered to, there is a good possibility of reaching a high-quality of green spaces for a multi-apartment residential complex.[38] This depends also on the shape and shading situation of green spaces, but to reach 8 m^2/inhabitant creates a high favorable situation.

Figure 4.18: Difference Between Green Space, Concentrated Green Space, and Open Space

a) Green Spaces　　**b) Concentrated Green Spaces**　　**c) Open Spaces**

☐ Project boundaries

Source: Asian Development Bank.

4.5.1　Sports Fields and Playgrounds

It is important to consider playgrounds and sports fields with adequate size, proportions, and arrangement when planning green spaces to support children's physical development. The space should offer various activities and all children should have diverse choices to play in and have fun.

Playgrounds designated for kindergarten-age children are recommended to be located at a distance of 5 m from buildings so that parents can comfortably watch over them. Such distance between playgrounds and residential spaces ensures adequate visibility and audibility. Playgrounds for older children are recommended to be located further from windows, at a distance of approximately 15 m, to avoid excessive noise.

The methodological guidelines for establishing the areas of sports fields and playgrounds are based on the experience of Berlin, as construction norms in Berlin provide clearer guidelines in this direction than in Tbilisi.[39] To establish the areas of sports fields and playgrounds,

---

38　Three big projects were also analyzed in Vienna: Sonnwendviertel, Nordbahnhof, and Seestadt. The main criteria for each block and land plot were analyzed. The average open space on the block level 8 m^2 per person and 4.5 m^2 green space per person.
39　Based on the communication with the Sports Department of the City Hall on different district offices, it is clear that there is no single standard being used for playgrounds and sports facilities.

the number of dwelling units in a residential development need to be considered. It is mandatory to build a playground if a residential building has more than six dwelling units. The minimum size of the playground should be 50 m^2. At minimum, 4 m^2 of the playground have to be envisaged for each dwelling unit. If 4 m^2 is divided by the number of persons within each household (the average number in Tbilisi–3.3), the total playground area per inhabitant is 1.2 m^2 (Box 4.11).[40]

It is important to plan small recreational spaces near residential buildings for those who have difficulties with movement or who cannot go to the neighborhood or district park for some other reasons. This is mainly true for elderly persons. Some like sitting facilities nearby playgrounds for young children, but others prefer more quiet situations (footnote 2).

Box 4.11: Analysis of the Playgrounds in the Study Area

Within the study area, the analysis of spatial indicators and capacity based on the data at hand on public playgrounds provided diverse and differing results. The area of playgrounds per inhabitant varies from 0.1 square meter to 2.08 square meters.

Sources: Tbilisi Transport and Urban Development Agency and ADB.

4.6 Access to Public Transportation and Parking

In the process of urban development, priority should be given to sustainable means of transportation, with a focus on public transportation, which will decrease dependence on private vehicles.

The planning process should take into consideration provision of equal spatial access to important city functions (work, education, recreation, cultural activities, etc.) and sustainable means of transportation for all citizens. Everyday movement or transportation routines of employees, caretakers, and housekeepers or homemakers vary by distance, number of destination points, and means of transportation. The trip chains within each of these routines should be as comfortable as possible. Therefore, public transport should offer a high level of quality in access to, speed, frequency, and reliability of the means of transportation, as well as availability of direct connections and capacity or busyness (Figure 4.19).

In Tbilisi, three main types of public transportation are designated as per catchment areas: transit (Tbilisi Bus Transit), subway, city, and neighborhood transportation.

---

[40] It is important to take into account that in Berlin and other European cities, the average household size is around 2.0 to 2.2. This means that the average playground area is bigger than in Tbilisi.

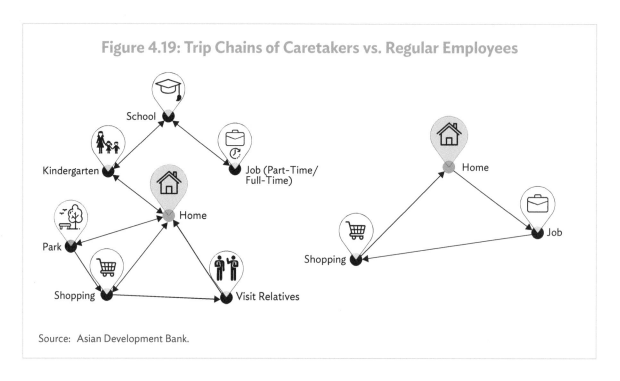

Figure 4.19: Trip Chains of Caretakers vs. Regular Employees

School

Kindergarten

Job (Part-Time/
Full-Time)

Home

Park

Shopping

Visit Relatives

Home

Shopping

Job

Source: Asian Development Bank.

Public transit transportation (Tbilisi Bus Transit, subway) is regarded as easily accessible on foot within 500 m from the place of residence. In city-level public transportation, this distance should not exceed 350 m. In neighborhood public transportation, this distance should be 200 m (Box 4.12).[41]

Accessibility and catchment areas of public transportation are directly linked to designing various functions at the level of a neighborhood or district. The logic of public transportation service areas should be considered when designing sites for shopping and commercial use. For example, shopping areas that have a rayon- or district- and city-wide importance should be located near a public transportation hub. District or neighborhood shopping areas should be located within the catchment area of district or neighborhood public transportation.

However, the street network hierarchy and functional service coverage or catchment areas have to be considered. Such functional diversity and activity are not recommended on all streets.

---

41   Transport and Urban Development Department at Tbilisi City Hall, 2021.

**Box 4.12: Pedestrian Accessibility to Public Transportation
from the Case Study Block**

A residential block selected within the study area has several types of public transportation available. A transit bus stop is accessible within the catchment area of 500 m, and a city-level public transportation stop is accessible within the catchment area of 350 m.

500 m
TBT

350 m
CITY

Research Area

Bus Stop

Sources: Tbilisi Transport and Urban Development Agency and ADB.

4.6.1 Parking Lots

Parking lots should not take up much of the ground-level space. A maximum 20% of the ground level should be used for the parking lots. If necessary, a separate building designated for parking lots can be planned. It is recommended that parking lot spaces are partially lit by daylight. The best solution is an arrangement in which people in the parking lot can be seen and heard from the outside.

The majority of ground-level space should be available for open public or semi-public spaces for joint usage, as well as green spaces.

APPENDIXES

Appendix 1: Additional Assessment Tools

Table A1.1: Assessment Matrix for the Qualitative Indicators

Project Title			
(Project site or the number of the block inside the project site)			
Thematic Blocks		**Criteria**	**Project Parameters** (On each block level or project site level)
Basic Information	1	Project area or block area (m^2) (–gross residential area)	
	2	Existing functional zones (m^2)	
	3	Proposed functional zones (m^2)	
	4	Net residential area (m^2) on ground floor	
	5	Proposed building coverage	
	6	Proposed floor area ratio (FAR) (net and gross)	
	7	Proposed green area ratio	
Density and Mixed Use	8	Gross floor space in total (m^2)	
	9	Net floor space for commerce use (m^2)	
	10	Net floor space for other uses (m^2)	
	11	Net floor space for residential use(m^2) (gross floor area: 20% and minus floor space of other functions)	
	12	Average size of (potential) dwelling unit (m^2)	
	13	Number of dwelling units (potential)	
	14	Potential inhabitants	
	15	Gross population density (inhabitant/ha) (calculated on gross residential area)	
Urban Structure	16	Maximum length and width of the block	
	17	Number of land plots	
	18	Maximum width of the building (m)	
	19	Number of floors	
	20	Area of the street network allocated as a separate land plot (m^2)	
	21	Length of the dead ends (m)	
	22	Dimension of the roundabout of the dead ends (maximum)	

continued on next page

Project Title			
(Project site or the number of the block inside the project site)			
Thematic Blocks		**Criteria**	**Project Parameters** (On each block level or project site level)
Social Infrastructure (Schools and Kindergartens)	23	Number of children of kindergarten age (2–5 years)	
	24	Distance (from home) of the next public kindergarten (m)	
	25	Land plot for the kindergarten (m)	
	26	Number of children of school age (6–19 years)	
	27	Distance (from home) to the next public school (m)	
	28	Land plot for school (m^2)	
Open and Green Spaces	29	Total area of open spaces including green space (m^2) and percentage of the project site (%)	
	30	Total area of green space (m^2) and percentage of the project site (%)	
	31	Concentrated green space (m^2) and percentage of the project site (%)	
	32	Open space per inhabitant (m^2/inhabitant)	
	33	Green space per inhabitant (m^2/inhabitant)	
	34	Concentrated green space per inhabitant (m^2/inhabitant)	
	35	Percentage of the concentrated green space sunlight (%) (taken on 1 April and 1 October at 11:00 a.m. and 3 p.m.)	
	36	Sports and playground area (m^2)	
Transport	37	Distance to the next public transport stop (m)	
	38	Number open parking spaces and the area they occupy on the ground (m^2) (%)	

ha = hectare, m^2 = square meter.
Source: Authors.

Table A1.2: Questionnaire to Assess Qualitative Indicators

How would you assess the quality of the residential development?	■ Is the floor area ratio (FAR) higher than acceptable, as people will perceive the density as too high? ■ What type of a structure does the development have (closed or partially open perimeter block, block with linear or high-rise buildings)? ■ Does the height of the building keep a human scale from street level or is the number of floors of the building more than six? ■ Does the planning structure ensure visual contact between dwelling units and public and semi-public open and green spaces? ■ Do the arrangement or location and dimensions of the buildings provide an opportunity to design well-lit dwelling units?
How comfortable is it for various groups to walk within the frames of the designed development?	■ Is the length of the block more than 150 meters and/or are the buildings perceived as barriers? ■ Are the walking routes free of barriers (for example, difference between levels, high dead or blank and long walls) and safe (is there sufficient social control and is the walking route visible and well-lit)? ■ Is the territory open–can it be accessed on foot and is it well-connected with the adjacent development?
How would you assess the quality of open and green spaces?	■ Are there sufficient open and green spaces within the urban morphology? ■ Does the location or arrangement and planning solutions of the buildings ensure formation of a unified concentrated space? ■ Does 40% of the concentrated green space have sufficient sunlight? ■ Are open and green spaces safe and easily accessible (free of barriers)? ■ Is there sufficient space between playgrounds and residential buildings to protect from the noise? ■ Are there playgrounds of sufficient size included? ■ Are playgrounds lit with sunlight? ■ If there is no concentrated green space included on the project territory, is there a public park within 250 meters of walking catchment area?
Are there any preconditions for functional diversity?	■ Are the main streets confined by buildings? ■ What is the percentage of the functional allocation of the ground level (street-level) floors? ■ Is the space left between the buildings along the main street and pedestrian movement wide enough for pedestrians to walk (this space does not include open parking lots and it should be at least 2.5 meters in the multi-apartment development)?

Source: Authors.

Appendix 2: Maps

The graphic data from the urban analysis of Vake neighborhood can be viewed electronically on the following link:

https://drive.google.com/file/d/1f3dpT3fi6Cxl4ZKTzbuBaYGt6sTK6ZTg/view.

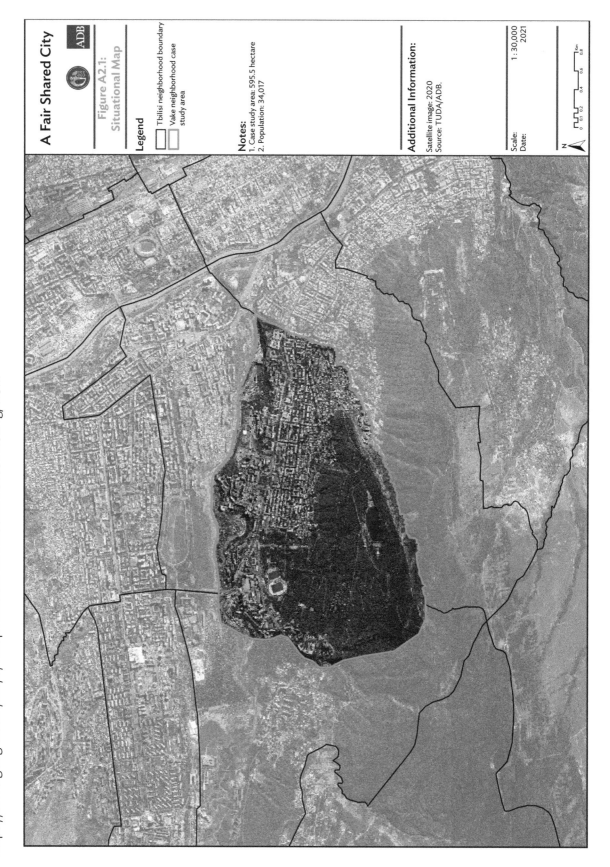

A Fair Shared City

Figure A2.1: Situational Map

Legend

☐ Tbilisi neighborhood boundary

☐ Vake neighborhood case study area

Notes:
1. Case study area: 595.5 hectare
2. Population: 34,017

Additional Information:

Satellite image: 2020
Source: TUDA/ADB.

Scale: 1 : 30,000
Date: 2021

N

0 0.1 0.2   0.4   0.6   0.8 Km

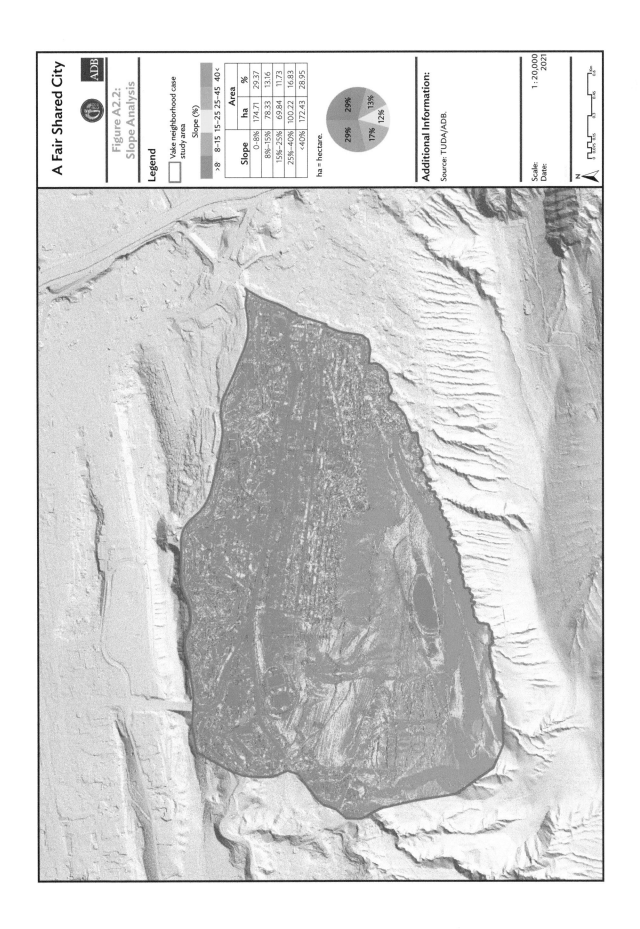

A Fair Shared City

Figure A2.2: Slope Analysis

Legend

☐ Vake neighborhood case study area

Slope (%)

>8   8-15   15-25   25-45   40<

Slope	Area	
	ha	%
0-8%	174.71	29.37
8%-15%	78.33	13.16
15%-25%	69.84	11.73
25%-40%	100.22	16.83
<40%	172.43	28.95

ha = hectare.

29%   29%   13%   17%   12%

Additional Information:

Source: TUDA/ADB.

Scale: 1:20,000
Date: 2021

N

0 0.075 0.15   0.3   0.45   0.6 km

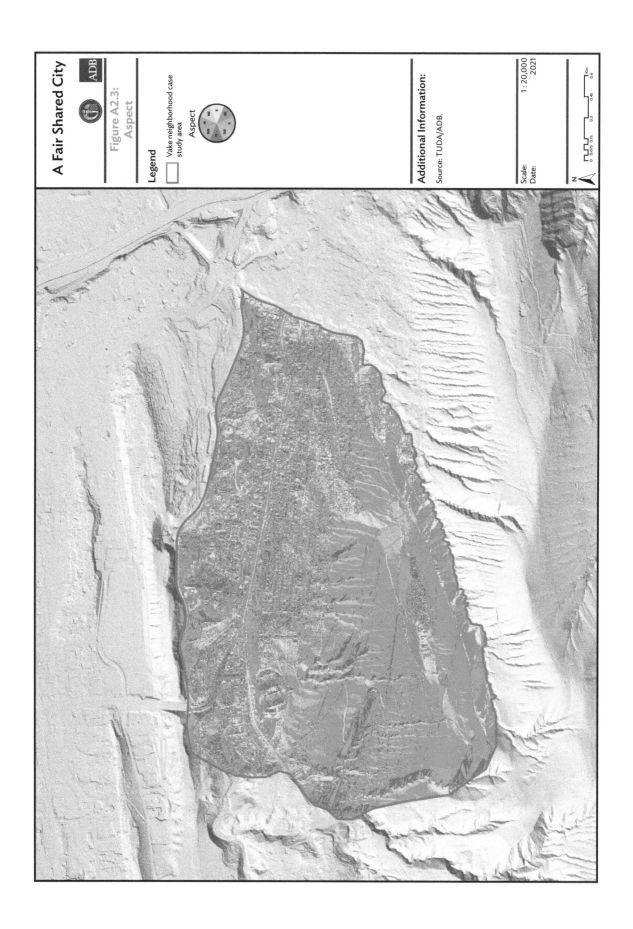

A Fair Shared City

Figure A2.3:
Aspect

Legend

☐ Vake neighborhood case
study area

Aspect

Additional Information:

Source: TUDA/ADB.

Scale: 1:20,000
Date: 2021

0 0.075 0.15   0.3   0.45   0.6 Km

N

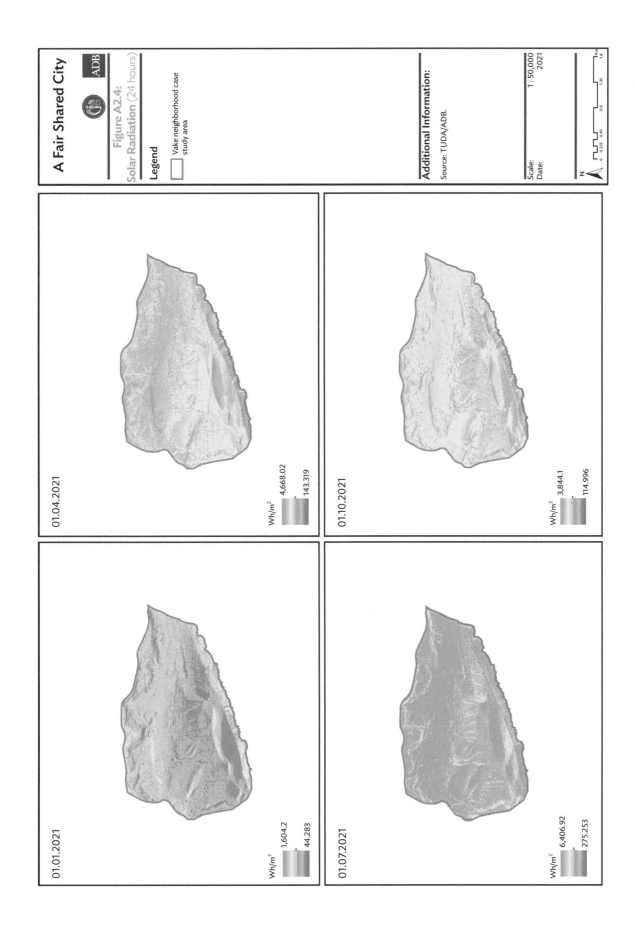

A Fair Shared City

ADB

Figure A2.4:
Solar Radiation (24 hours)

Legend

Vake neighborhood case
study area

Additional Information:

Source: TUDA/ADB.

Scale: 1 : 50,000
Date: 2021

N

0   0.225 0.45   0.9   1.35   1.8 Km

01.04.2021

Wh/m²   4,668.02

143.319

01.10.2021

Wh/m²   3,844.1

114.996

01.01.2021

Wh/m²   1,604.2

44.283

01.07.2021

Wh/m²   6,406.92

275.253

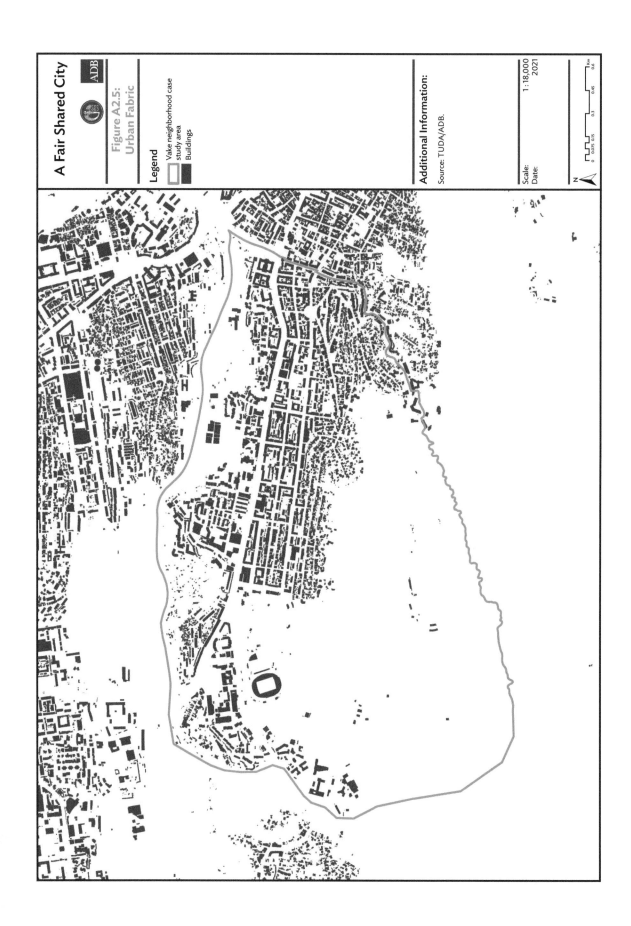

A Fair Shared City

Figure A2.5:
Urban Fabric

Legend

☐ Vake neighborhood case
study area

■ Buildings

Additional Information:

Source: TUDA/ADB.

Scale: 1 : 18,000
Date: 2021

0 0.075 0.15   0.3   0.45   0.6 km

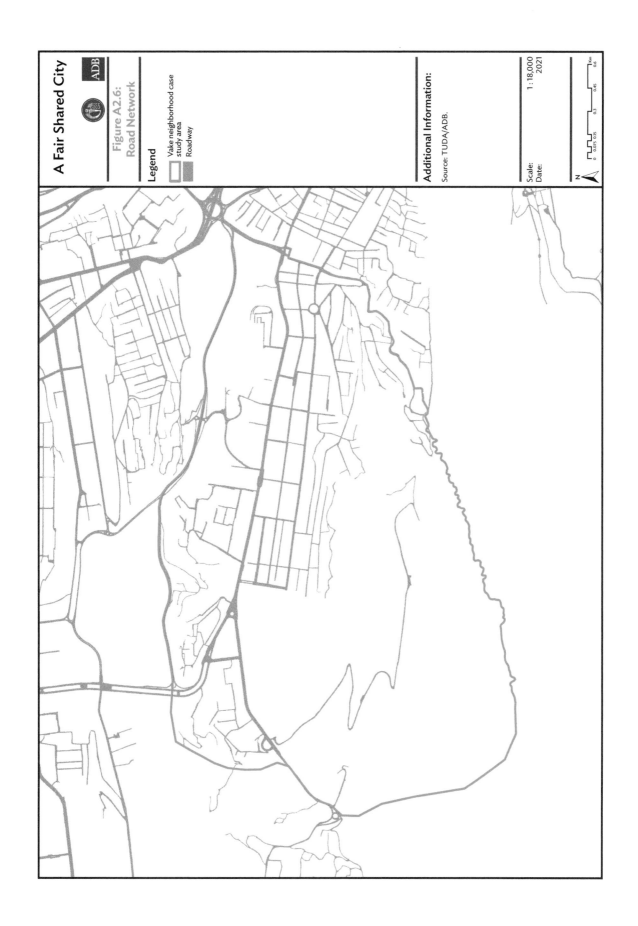

A Fair Shared City

**Figure A2.6:
Road Network**

Legend

☐ Vake neighborhood case
study area

▨ Roadway

Additional Information:

Source: TUDA/ADB.

Scale: 1 : 18,000
Date: 2021

N

0 0.075 0.15   0.3   0.45   0.6 km

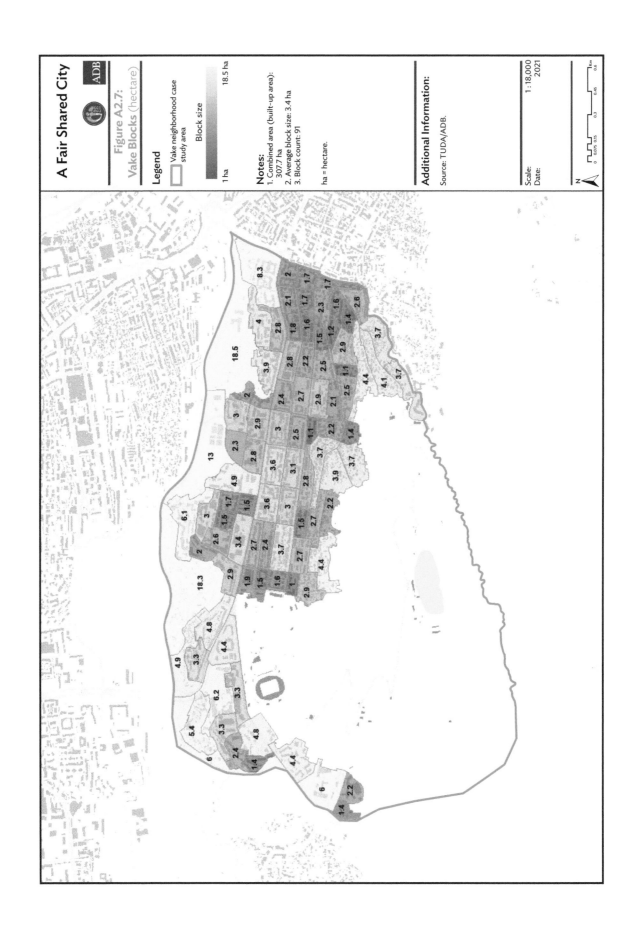

A Fair Shared City

Figure A2.7:
Vake Blocks (hectare)

Legend

☐ Vake neighborhood case study area

Block size

1 ha — 18.5 ha

Notes:
1. Combined area (built-up area): 307.7 ha
2. Average block size: 3.4 ha
3. Block count: 91

ha = hectare.

Additional Information:

Source: TUDA/ADB.

Scale: 1:18,000
Date: 2021

0 0.075 0.15   0.3   0.45   0.6   Km

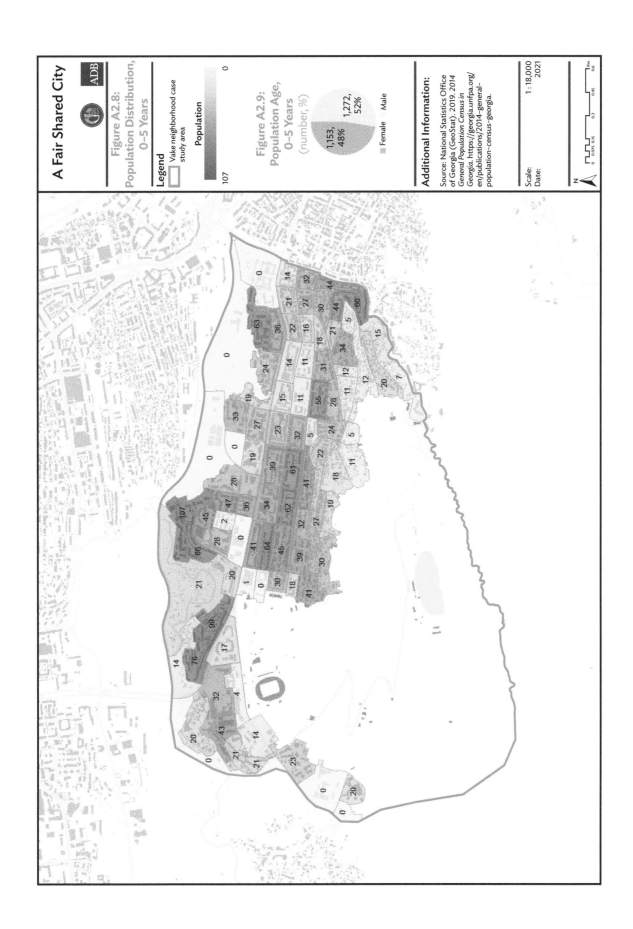

A Fair Shared City

Figure A2.8:
Population Distribution,
0–5 Years

Legend

☐ Vake neighborhood case
study area

Population

107 ▮▮▮▮▮ 0

Figure A2.9:
Population Age,
0–5 Years
(number, %)

1,153,
48%   1,272,
       52%

▮ Female ▮ Male

Additional Information:

Source: National Statistics Office
of Georgia (GeoStat). 2019. 2014
General Population Census in
Georgia. https://georgia.unfpa.org/
en/publications/2014-general-
population-census-georgia.

Scale: 1 : 18,000
Date: 2021

N

0 0.025 0.15   0.3   0.45   0.6 Km

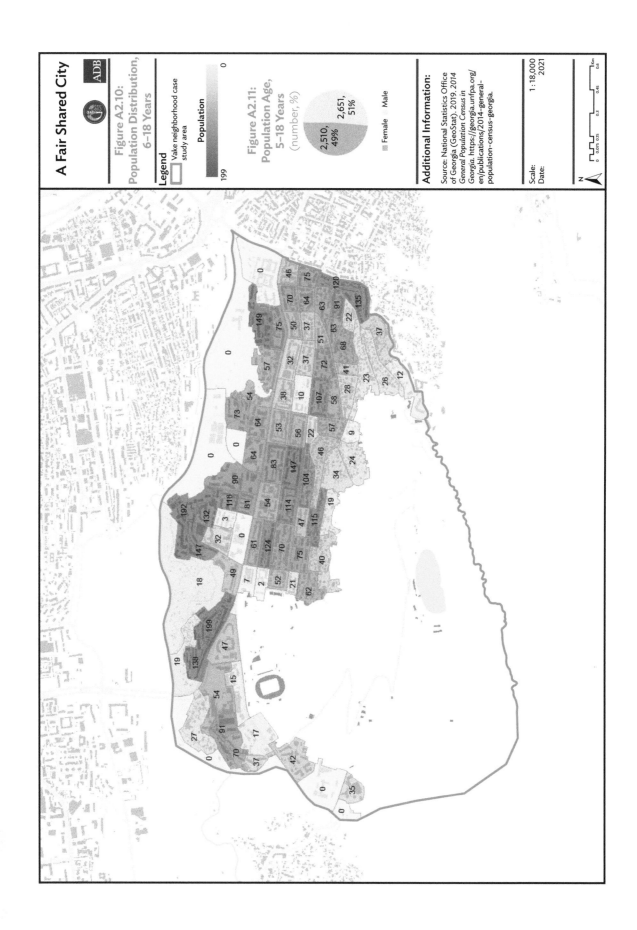

A Fair Shared City

Figure A2.10:
Population Distribution,
6–18 Years

Legend

☐ Vake neighborhood case
study area

Population

199
0

Figure A2.11:
Population Age,
5–18 Years
(number, %)

2,510,
49%

2,651,
51%

■ Female ■ Male

Additional Information:

*Source: National Statistics Office
of Georgia (GeoStat). 2019. 2014
General Population Census in
Georgia. https://georgia.unfpa.org/
en/publications/2014-general-
population-census-georgia.*

Scale: 1 : 18,000
Date: 2021

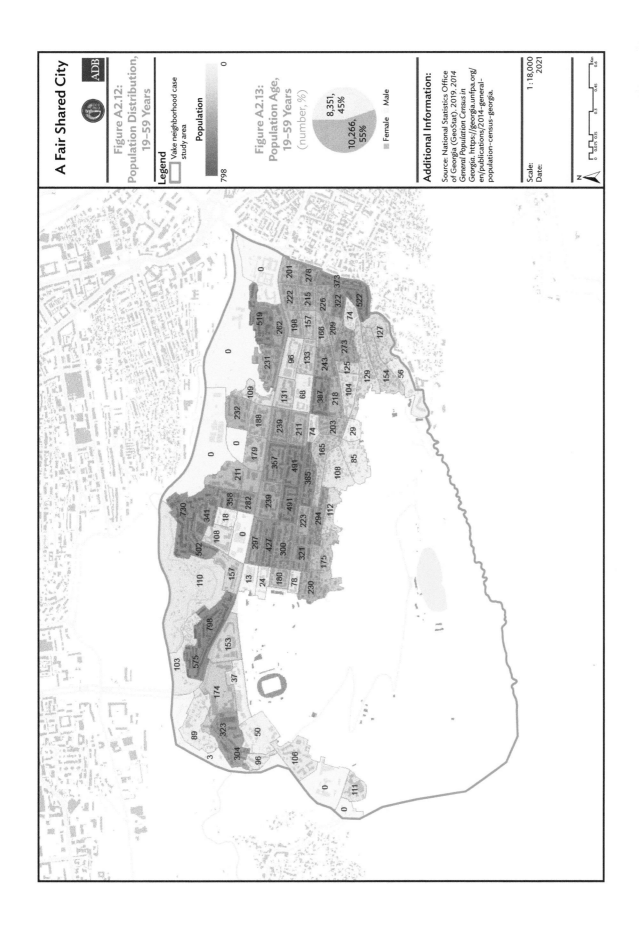

A Fair Shared City

Figure A2.12:
Population Distribution,
19–59 Years

Legend

Vake neighborhood case
study area

Population

0

798

Figure A2.13:
Population Age,
19–59 Years
(number, %)

8,351,
45%

10,266,
55%

Female   Male

Additional Information:

Source: National Statistics Office
of Georgia (GeoStat). 2019. 2014
General Population Census in
Georgia. https://georgia.unfpa.org/
en/publications/2014-general-
population-census-georgia.

Scale: 1:18,000
Date: 2021

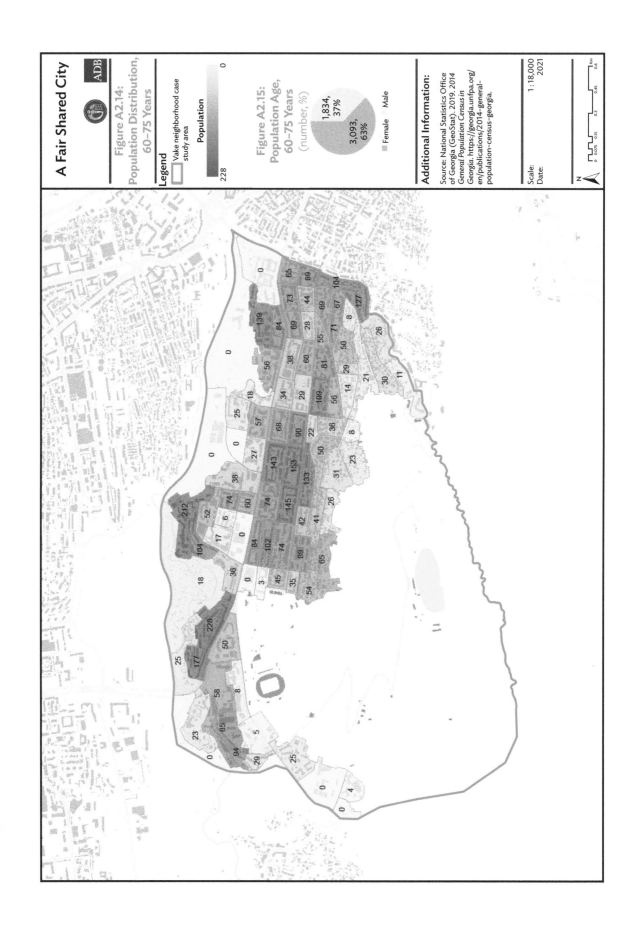

A Fair Shared City

Figure A2.14: Population Distribution, 60–75 Years

Legend

☐ Vake neighborhood case study area

Population

228
0

Figure A2.15: Population Age, 60–75 Years

(number, %)

3,093, 63%
1,834, 37%

■ Female   ■ Male

Additional Information:

Source: National Statistics Office of Georgia (GeoStat). 2019. *2014 General Population Census in Georgia.* https://georgia.unfpa.org/en/publications/2014-general-population-census-georgia.

Scale: 1:18,000
Date: 2021

0 0.075 0.15 0.3 0.45 0.6 Km

N

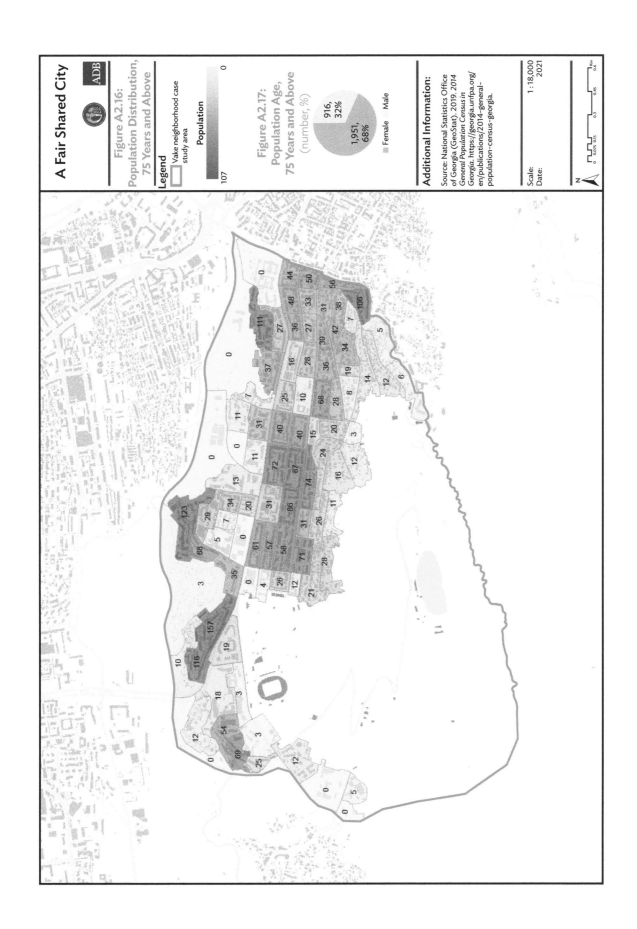

A Fair Shared City

Figure A2.16:
Population Distribution,
75 Years and Above

Legend

☐ Vake neighborhood case
study area

Population

107 ▬▬▬▬ 0

Figure A2.17:
Population Age,
75 Years and Above
(number, %)

916,
32%

1,951,
68%

■ Female ■ Male

Additional Information:

Source: National Statistics Office
of Georgia (GeoStat). 2019. 2014
General Population Census in
Georgia. https://georgia.unfpa.org/
en/publications/2014-general-
population-census-georgia.

Scale: 1:18,000
Date: 2021

0 0.075 0.15   0.3   0.45   0.6
Km

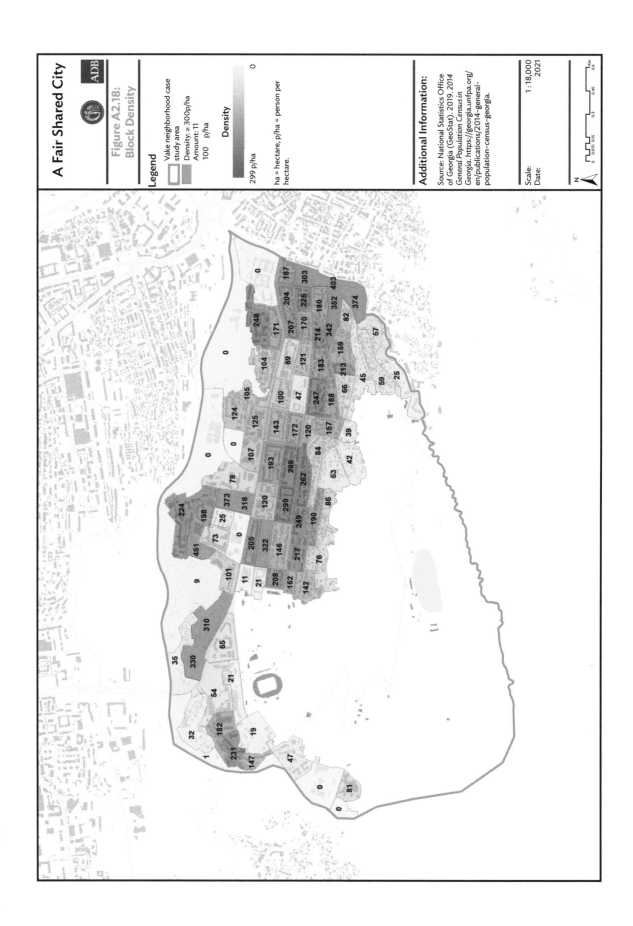

A Fair Shared City

Figure A2.18:
Block Density

Legend

Vake neighborhood case
study area
Density: ≥ 300p/ha
Amount: 11
100   p/ha

Density

0

299 p/ha

ha = hectare, p/ha = person per
hectare.

Additional Information:

Source: National Statistics Office
of Georgia (GeoStat), 2019, 2014
General Population Census in
Georgia. https://georgia.unfpa.org/
en/publications/2014-general-
population-census-georgia.

Scale: 1:18,000
Date: 2021

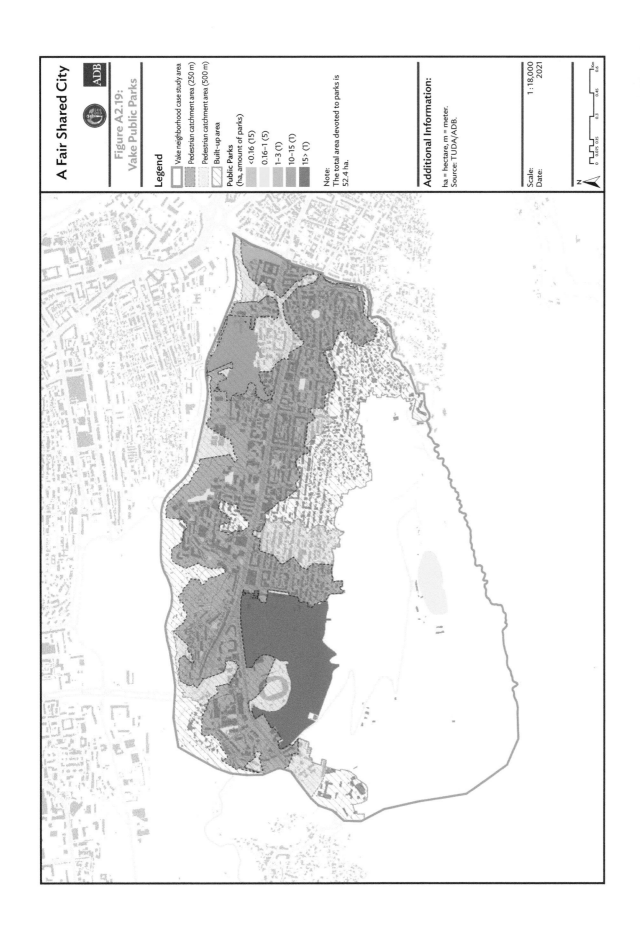

A Fair Shared City

Figure A2.19:
Vake Public Parks

Legend

☐ Vake neighborhood case study area
Pedestrian catchment area (250 m)
Pedestrian catchment area (500 m)
Built-up area

Public Parks
(ha, amount of parks)
<0.16 (15)
0.16–1 (5)
1–3 (1)
10–15 (1)
15> (1)

Note:
The total area devoted to parks is
52.4 ha.

Additional Information:

ha = hectare, m = meter.
Source: TUDA/ADB.

Scale: 1 : 18,000
Date: 2021

N

0   0.075 0.15   0.3   0.45   0.6

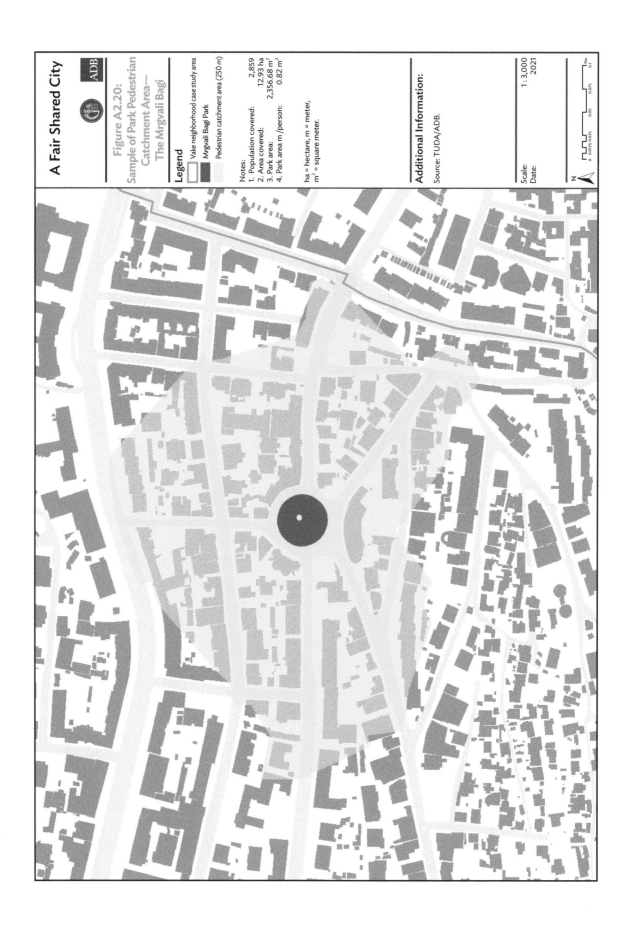

A Fair Shared City

Figure A2.20:
Sample of Park Pedestrian Catchment Area—The Mrgvali Bagi

Legend

☐ Vake neighborhood case study area
■ Mrgvali Bagi Park
▨ Pedestrian catchment area (250 m)

Notes:
1. Population covered: 2,859
2. Area covered: 12.93 ha
3. Park area: 2,356.68 m²
4. Park area m /person: 0.82 m²

ha = hectare, m = meter,
m² = square meter.

Additional Information:

Source: TUDA/ADB.

Scale: 1:3,000
Date: 2021

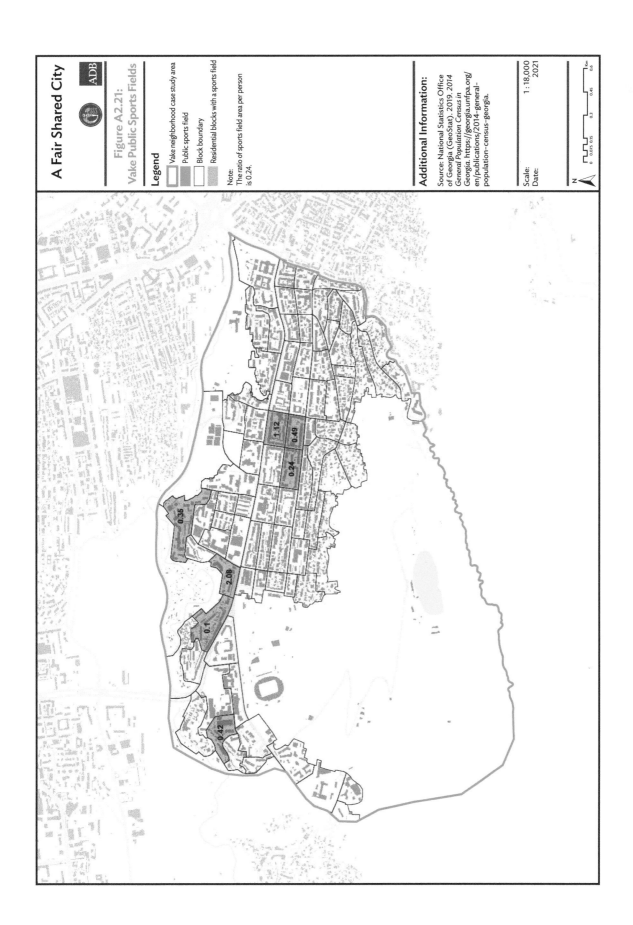

A Fair Shared City

Figure A2.21:
Vake Public Sports Fields

Legend

☐ Vake neighborhood case study area
▨ Public sports field
☐ Block boundary
▨ Residential blocks with a sports field

Note:
The ratio of sports field area per person
is 0.24.

Additional Information:

Source: National Statistics Office
of Georgia (GeoStat). 2019. *2014
General Population Census in
Georgia.* https://georgia.unfpa.org/
en/publications/2014-general-
population-census-georgia.

Scale: 1 : 18,000
Date: 2021

0   0.075 0.15   0.3   0.45   0.6
                                          Km

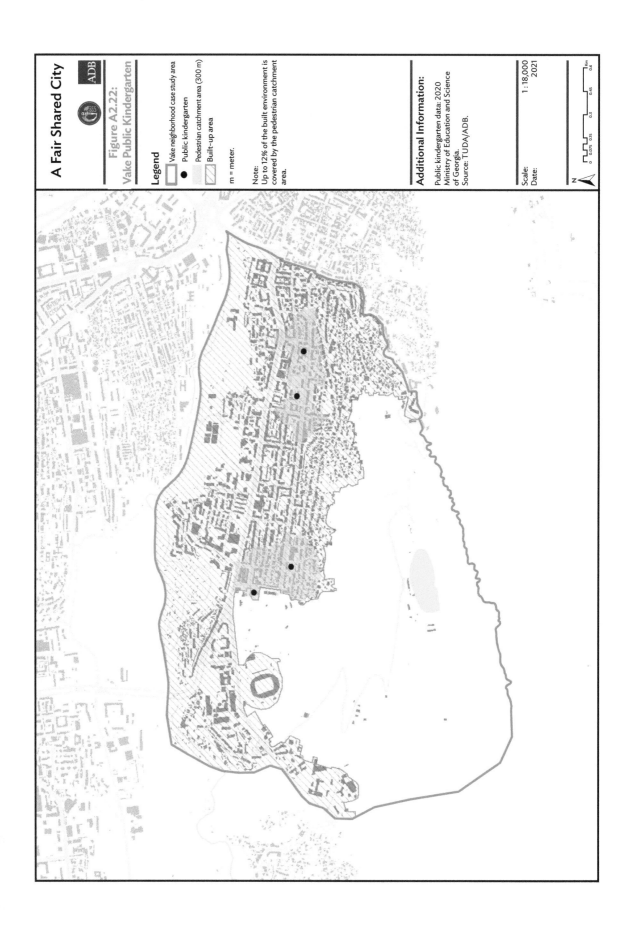

A Fair Shared City

Figure A2.22:
Vake Public Kindergarten

Legend

☐ Vake neighborhood case study area
● Public kindergarten
▨ Pedestrian catchment area (300 m)
▨ Built-up area

m = meter.

Note:
Up to 12% of the built environment is covered by the pedestrian catchment area.

Additional Information:

Public kindergarten data: 2020
Ministry of Education and Science
of Georgia.
Source: TUDA/ADB.

Scale: 1 : 18,000
Date: 2021

0   0.075 0.15   0.3   0.45   0.6
Km

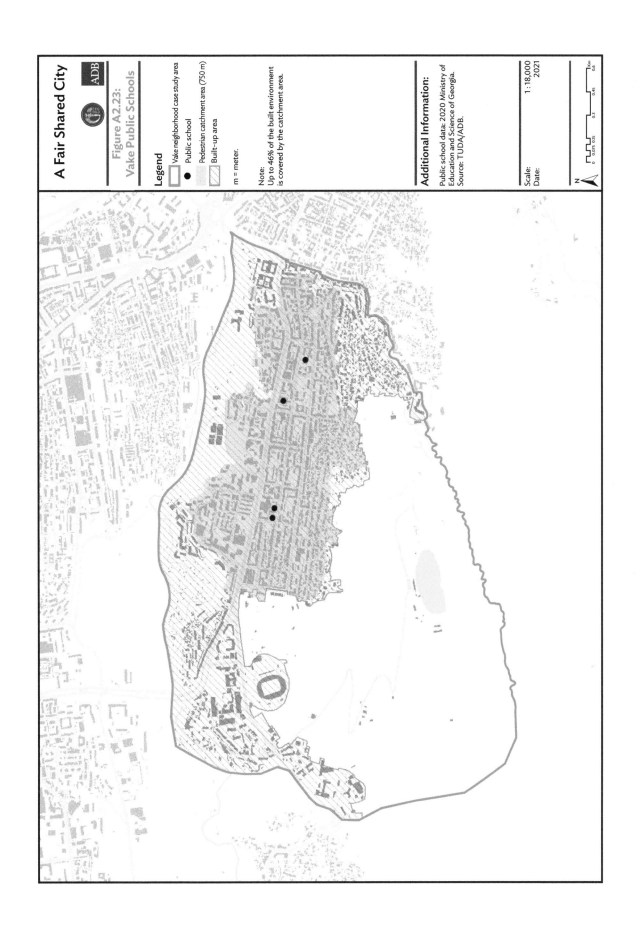

A Fair Shared City

ADB

Figure A2.23:
Vake Public Schools

Legend

☐ Vake neighborhood case study area

● Public school

▨ Pedestrian catchment area (750 m)

▨ Built-up area

m = meter.

Note:
Up to 46% of the built environment
is covered by the catchment area.

Additional Information:

Public school data: 2020 Ministry of
Education and Science of Georgia.
Source: TUDA/ADB.

Scale: 1 : 18,000
Date: 2021

N

0 0.075 0.15   0.3   0.45   0.6 Km

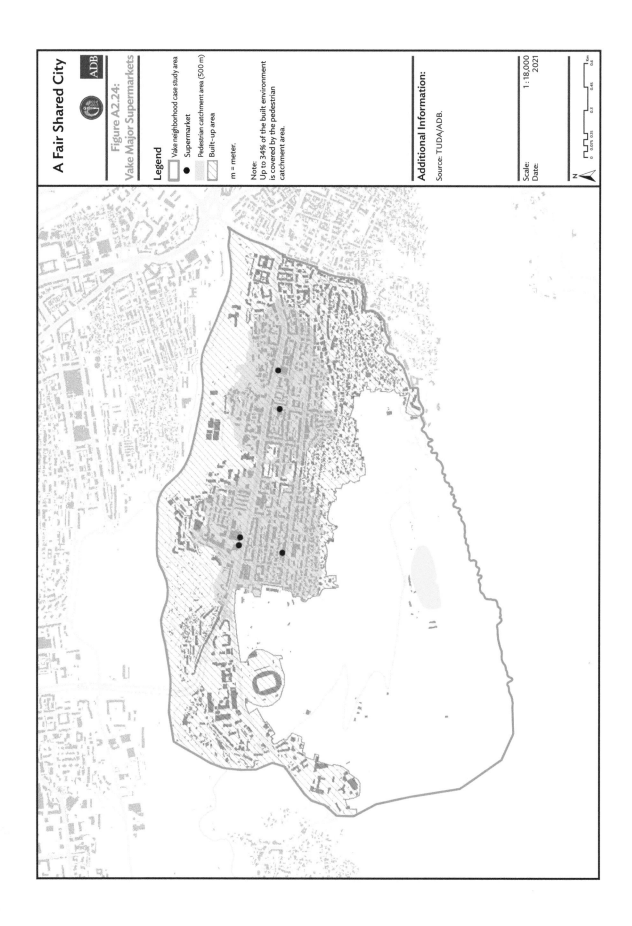

A Fair Shared City

Figure A2.24:
Vake Major Supermarkets

Legend

☐ Vake neighborhood case study area
● Supermarket
▨ Pedestrian catchment area (500 m)
▨ Built-up area

m = meter.

Note:
Up to 34% of the built environment
is covered by the pedestrian
catchment area.

Additional Information:

Source: TUDA/ADB.

Scale: 1:18,000
Date: 2021

N

0 0.075 0.15   0.3   0.45   0.6
                              Km

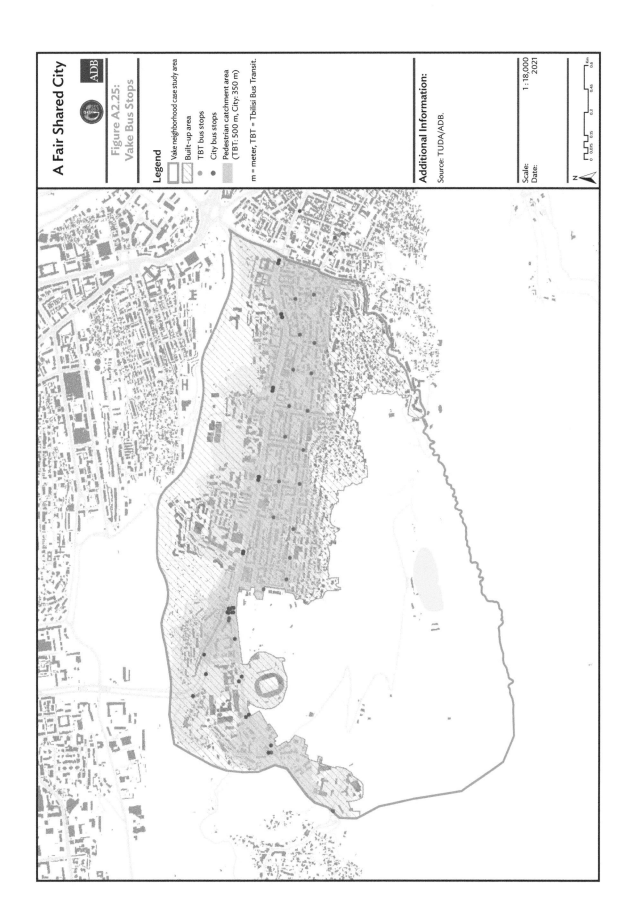

A Fair Shared City

Figure A2.25:
Vake Bus Stops

Legend

▢ Vake neighborhood case study area
▨ Built-up area
• TBT bus stops
• City bus stops
▨ Pedestrian catchment area
(TBT: 500 m, City: 350 m)

m = meter, TBT = Tbilisi Bus Transit.

Additional Information:

Source: TUDA/ADB.

Scale: 1 : 18,000
Date: 2021

Km
0 0.075 0.15   0.3   0.45   0.6

N

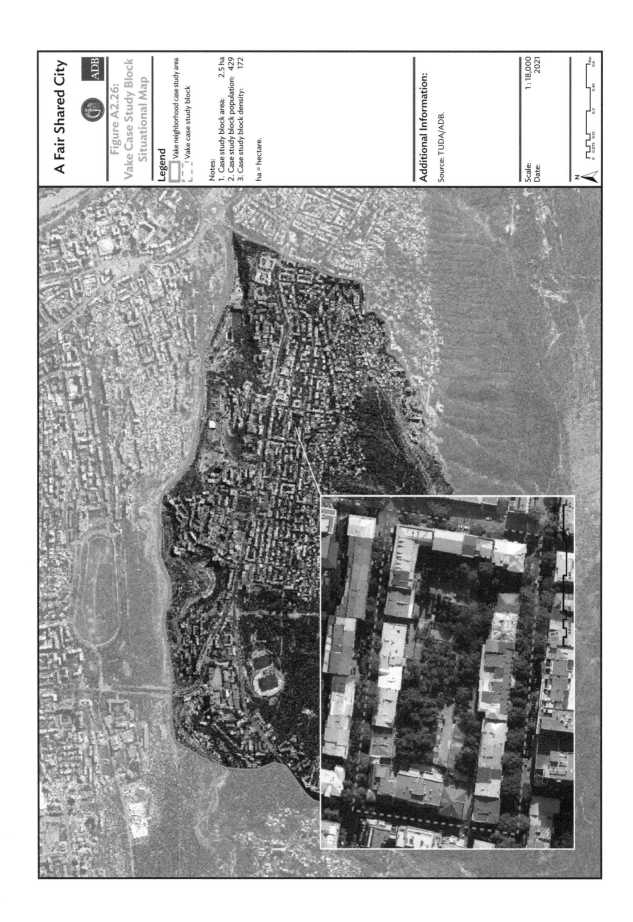

A Fair Shared City

Figure A2.26:
Vake Case Study Block
Situational Map

Legend

☐ Vake neighborhood case study area

⌐ ¬ Vake case study block
L _ ┘

Notes:
1. Case study block area: 2.5 ha
2. Case study block population: 429
3. Case study block density: 172

ha = hectare.

Additional Information:

Source: TUDA/ADB.

Scale: 1:18,000
Date: 2021

0 0.075 0.15   0.3   0.45   0.6 km

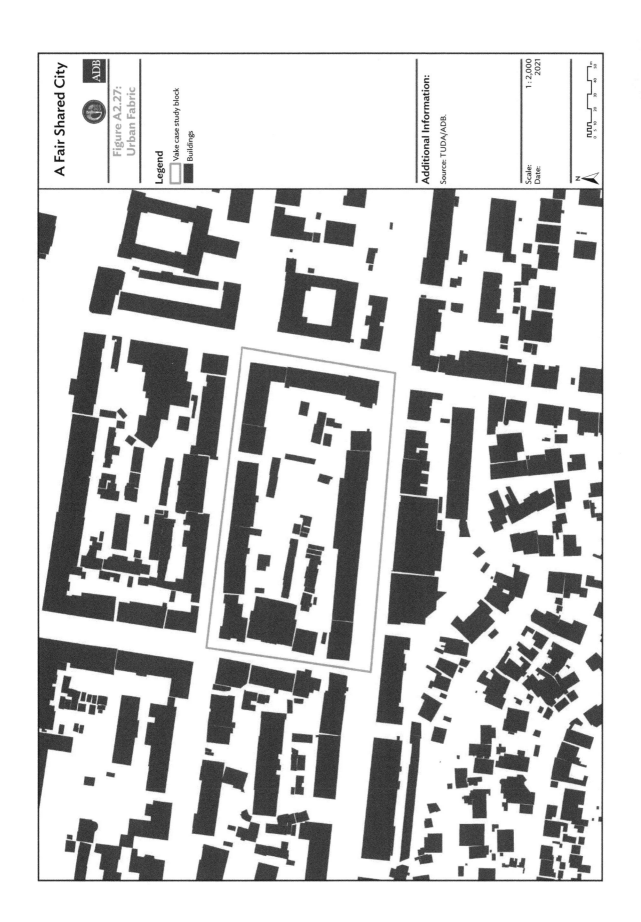

A Fair Shared City

ADB

Figure A2.27:
Urban Fabric

Legend

☐ Vake case study block

■ Buildings

Additional Information:

Source: TUDA/ADB.

Scale: 1 : 2,000
Date: 2021

N

0 5 10 20 30 40 50 m

83

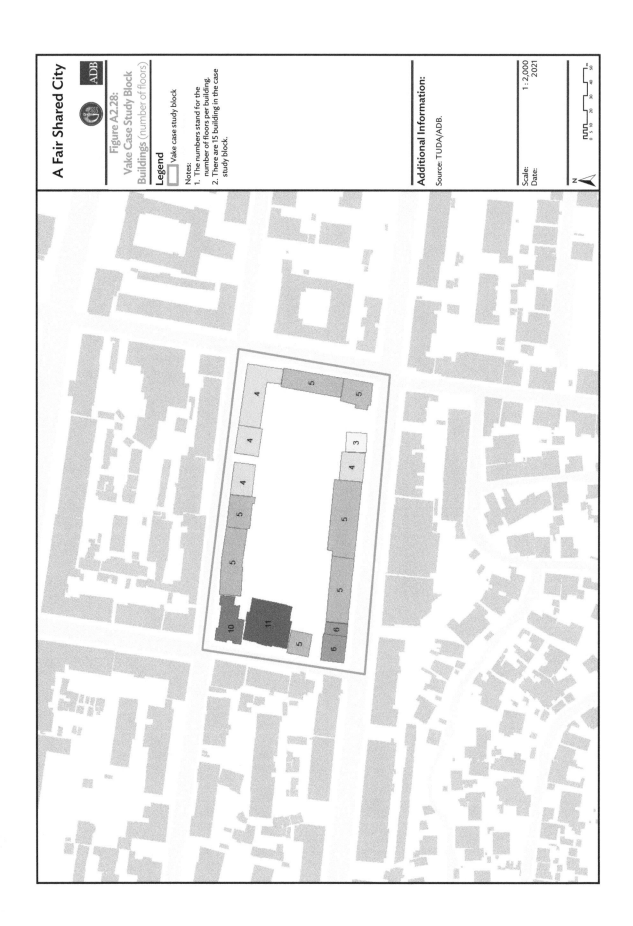

A Fair Shared City

Figure A2.28:
Vake Case Study Block
Buildings (number of floors)

Legend
☐ Vake case study block

Notes:
1. The numbers stand for the number of floors per building.
2. There are 15 building in the case study block.

Additional Information:

Source: TUDA/ADB.

Scale: 1 : 2,000
Date: 2021

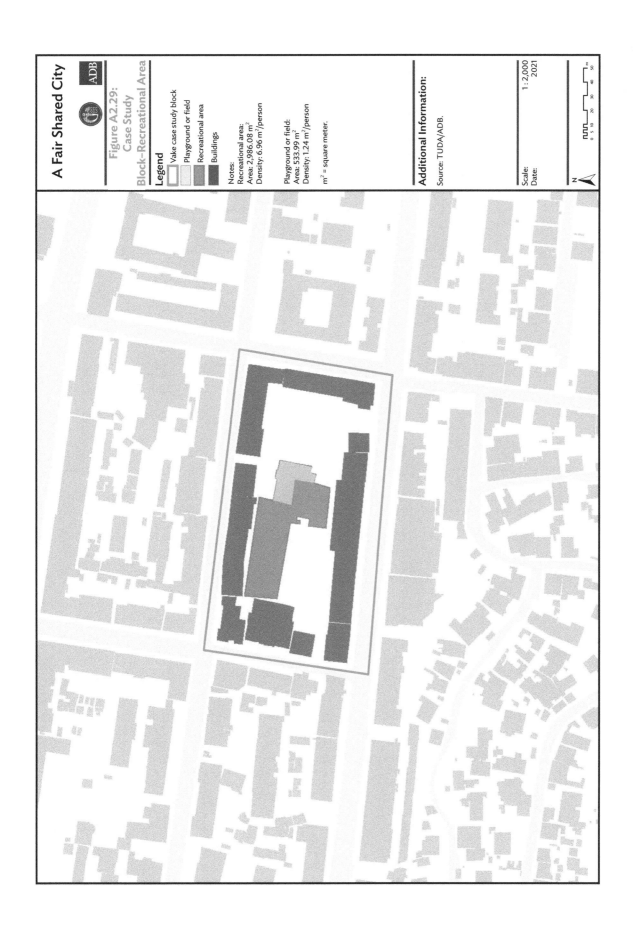

A Fair Shared City

Figure A2.29:
Case Study
Block–Recreational Area

Legend

☐ Vake case study block
☐ Playground or field
☐ Recreational area
■ Buildings

Notes:
Recreational area:
Area: 2,986.08 m²
Density: 6.96 m²/person

Playground or field:
Area: 533.99 m²
Density: 1.24 m²/person

m² = square meter.

Additional Information:

Source: TUDA/ADB.

Scale: 1 : 2,000
Date: 2021

N

0 5 10   20   30   40   50
                                  m

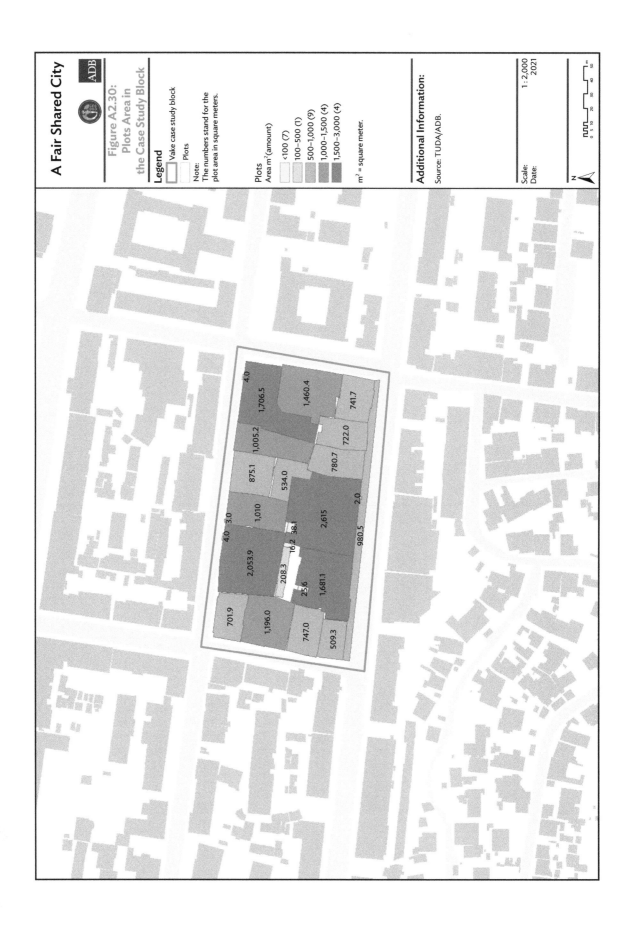

A Fair Shared City

Figure A2.30:
Plots Area in
the Case Study Block

Legend

▢ Vake case study block

▢ Plots

Note:
The numbers stand for the
plot area in square meters.

Plots
Area m² (amount)
▢ <100 (7)
▢ 100–500 (1)
▢ 500–1,000 (9)
▢ 1,000–1,500 (4)
▢ 1,500–3,000 (4)

m² = square meter.

Additional Information:

Source: TUDA/ADB.

Scale: 1 : 2,000
Date: 2021

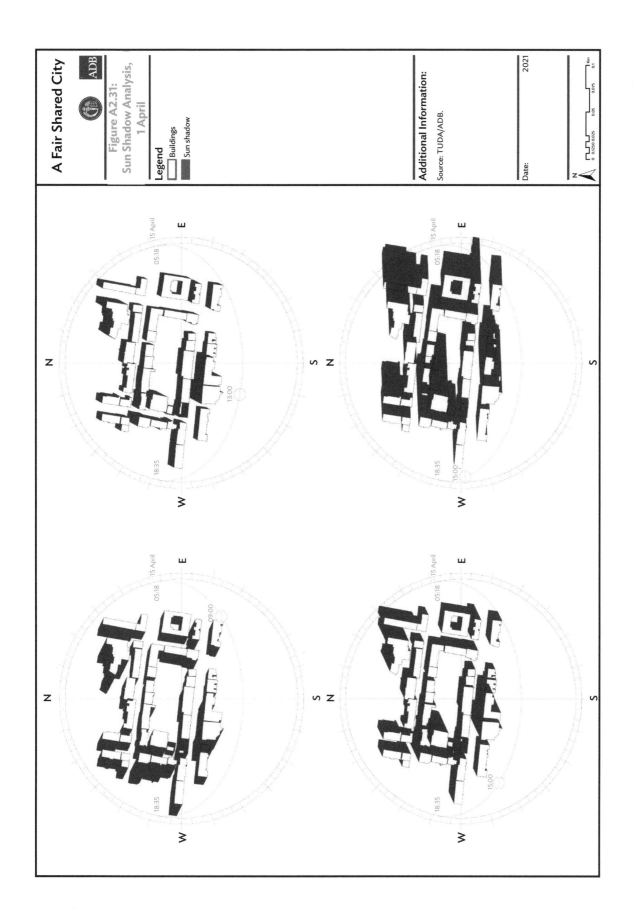

A Fair Shared City

Figure A2.31:
Sun Shadow Analysis,
1 April

Legend
☐ Buildings
■ Sun shadow

Additional Information:

Source: TUDA/ADB.

Date: 2021

N

0 0.0250 0.025   0.05   0.075   0.1 Km

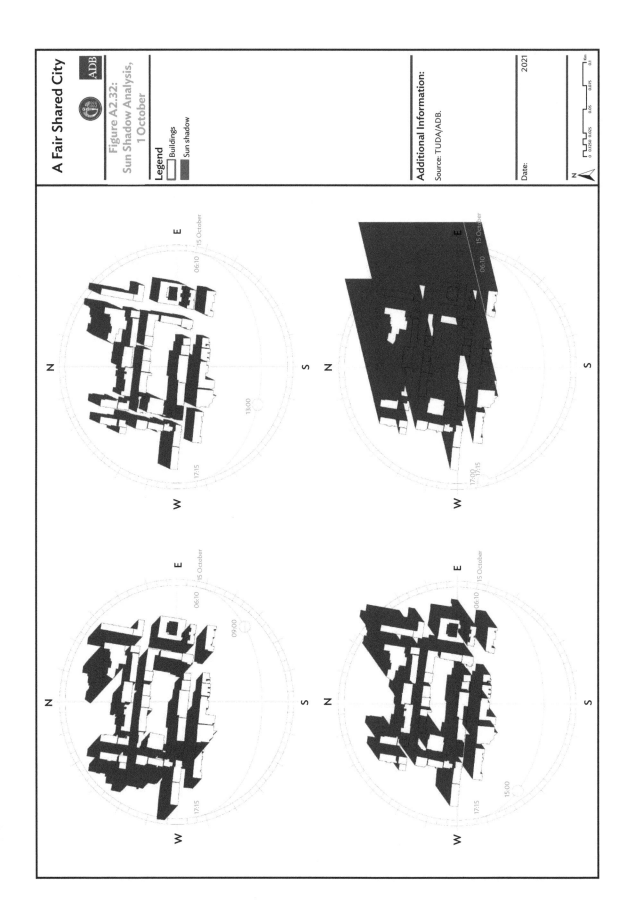

A Fair Shared City

Figure A2.32:
Sun Shadow Analysis,
1 October

Legend

☐ Buildings
■ Sun shadow

Additional Information:

Source: TUDA/ADB.

Date: 2021

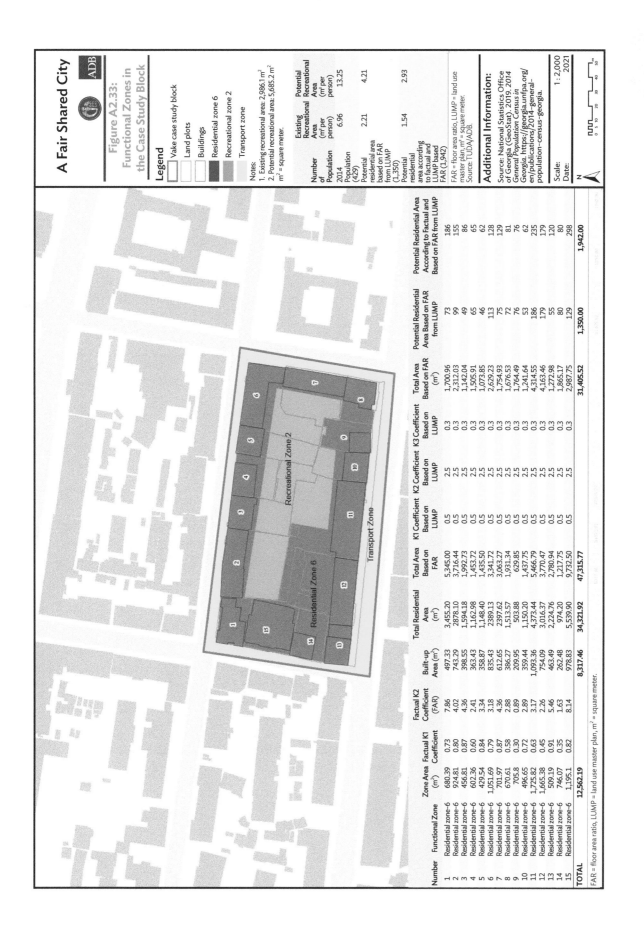

A Fair Shared City

Figure A2.33: Functional Zones in the Case Study Block

REFERENCES

ADB and Tbilisi City Hall. 2021. *Fair Shared Green and Recreational Spaces: Guidelines for Gender-Responsive and Inclusive Design.* Manila. https://www.adb.org/sites/default/files/publication/762081/green-spaces-guidelines-gender-responsive-design-tbilisi.pdf.

ADB and the Government of Georgia, Ministry of Regional Development and Infrastructure. Forthcoming. Inclusive Urban Area Guidelines.

Alexander, C. et al. 1977. *A Pattern Language: Towns, Buildings, Construction.* New York: Oxford University Press.

ArchDaily. 2020. *Querbeet Social Housing / Synn Architekten.* https://www.archdaily.com/934266/querbeet-social-housing-synn-architekten-zt-og.

ADB. 2010. *Report and Recommendation of the President to the Board of Directors: Proposed Loan to Georgia for the Sustainable Urban Transport Investment Program.* Manila (Loan 2655).

ADB. 2014. *Technical Assistance for Promoting Gender Equality and Women's Empowerment Phase 2:* Future Cities Future Women Phase 1. Manila (TA 8797-REG).

ADB. 2015. *Green City Development Tool Kit.* Manila:. https://www.adb.org/sites/default/files/institutional-document/173693/green-city-dev-toolkit.pdf

ADB. 2016. *Technical Assistance to Georgia for Livable Urban Areas: Integrated Urban Plans for Balanced Regional Development.* Manila (TA 9220-GEO).

ADB. 2017. Technical Assistance for Strengthening Institutions for Localizing Agenda 2030 for Sustainable Development. Manila (TA 9387-REG).

ADB. 2017. *Enabling Inclusive Cities: Toolkit for Inclusive Urban Development.* Manila. https://www.adb.org/documents/enabling-inclusive-cities

ADB. 2019. *Report and Recommendation of the President to the Board of Directors: Proposed Loan to Georgia for the Livable Cities Investment Program.* Manila (Loan 6024-GEO).

ADB. 2021. *Creating Livable Asian Cities*. Manila.. https://www.adb.org/publications/creating-livable-asian-cities.

City of Vienna, MA-18 – Urban Development and Planning. 2013. *Gender Mainstreaming in Urban Planning and Urban Development*. Vienna. https://www.wien.gv.at/stadtentwicklung/studien/pdf/b008358.pdf.

Gehl, J. 2010. *Cities for People*. Washington, DC: Island Press.

Government of Georgia, Ministry of Education, Science, Culture and Sports. 4 November 2020 (Letter MES 1 20 0001066371).

Government of Georgia, Ministry of Education, Science, Culture and Sports. 22 March 2021 (Letter MES 8 21 0000267131).

Government of Georgia, Ministry of Labor, Health and Social Affairs. 2001. Order No. 308: On the Approval of Arrangement, Equipment and Sanitary Rules and Norms of Pre-School and General Education Institutions.

Government of Georgia, National Statistics Office. General Population Census of 2014.

Government of Georgia, National Statistics Office. 2 December 2020. Letter N9-2740.

Government of Georgia. State Sub-Department of the Ministry of Internal Affairs to Emergency Management Service. 22 February 2021 (Letter MIA 7 21 00428069).

Legislative Herald of Georgia. 2019. On the Rules for Developing Spatial and City Planning Documentation. Decree No. 260. Government of Georgia . https://matsne.gov.ge/en/document/view/4579368?publication=0 (accessed 21 May 2021).

Legislative Herald of Georgia. 2016. Regulations on the Usage and Development of Territories in Tbilisi Municipality. Decree No. 14- 19. Tbilisi City Assembly. https://matsne.gov.ge/ en/document/view/3292207?publication=0.

Legislative Herald of Georgia. 2019. The Land Use Master Plan of the Capital City. Decree No. 18-39. Tbilisi City Assembly. https://matsne.gov.ge/document/ view/4508064?publication=0.

Legislative Herald of Georgia. 2016. Technical Rules for the Safety of Constructions and Buildings. Decree No. 41. Government of Georgia. https://matsne.gov.ge/en/document/view/3176389?publication=0.

Mercer. 2019. Quality of Living City Ranking. https://mobilityexchange.mercer.com/insights/quality-of- living-rankings

Sandhu, S. et al. 2016. *GREEEN Solutions for Livable Cities*. Manila: Asian Development Bank. https://www.adb.org/sites/default/files/publication/181442/greeen-solutions-livable-cities.pdf.

Systra. 2016. *Consulting Services for Organization of a Transportation Household Survey in Tbilisi Metropolitan Area*. ADB, Municipal Development Fund of Georgia, and Tbilisi City Hall. https://tbilisi.gov.ge/img/original/2018/4/20/THS_Final_Report_Eng.pdf.

Tbilisi City Assembly. Kakheti Highway. Decree No. 238.. 2020.

UN-Habitat. 2021. *A New Strategy of Sustainable Neighbourhood Planning: Five Principles*. Discussion Note 3. Nairobi. https://unhabitat.org/a-new-strategy-of-sustainable-neighbourhood-planning-five-principles

Urban Design Alliance. 2007. *Urban Design Compendium*. London: English Partnerships and The Housing Corporation. https://webapps.stoke.gov.uk/uploadedfiles/Urban%20Design%20Compendium%201.pdf.

References

Lightning Source UK Ltd.
Milton Keynes UK
UKHW051239100622
404218UK00012B/131